1. St. Margaret Mary

SAINT MARGARET MARY AND THE PROMISES OF THE SACRED HEART

Saint Margaret Mary Alacoque and the Promises of the Sacred Heart

By Msgr. Leon Cristiani

Translated from the French
by M. Angeline Bouchard

St. Paul Editions

Imprimatur:
+Humberto Cardinal Medeiros
Archbishop of Boston

June 6, 1974

Original French title: "Sainte Marguerite-Marie et les Promesses du Sacre-Coeur"

NIHIL OBSTAT
Ch. Cordonnier

IMPRIMATUR
Pierre Girard, S.S., V.G.

Grateful acknowledgment is made to *The Pope Speaks* (TPS), Church Documents Quarterly, 3622 Twelfth St. N.E., Washington, D.C. 20017, for their translation of the Encyclical Letter on Devotion to the Sacred Heart.

Library of Congress Catalog Card Number: 74-16748

Printed in U.S.A. by the Daughters of St. Paul
50 St. Paul's Ave., Boston, Ma. 02130

The Daughters of St. Paul are an international religious congregation serving the Church with the communications media.

CONTENTS

Introduction

The name of St. Margaret Mary is inseparable from devotion to the Sacred Heart. Certainly, this devotion existed long before her. Indeed, it can be traced back to the earliest Christian times, and is rooted in the Gospel itself. If this were not so, it could never have been implanted in the Church. For it has wisely been said that the Church innovates only with what is ancient.

Margaret Mary could never have invented devotion to the Sacred Heart. It would even be false to claim her private revelations were the real source of this devotion. For private revelations can add nothing to Revelation in the strict sense of the word, the latter having been closed with the death of St. John, the last of the apostles to survive. The apparitions at Paray-le-Monial were only an occasion for rekindling Christian devotion. Theologians had to make careful inquiry into the substance of Margaret Mary's private revelations. In the last instance, the Church officially established public worship of the Sacred Heart. Its supreme magisterium introduced the feast of the Sacred Heart into the liturgy, and recommended devotion to the Sacred Heart to all the faithful in numerous documents which explained its nature, importance, and inexhaustible riches.

Besides, the Church has acknowledged that the little French nun of the Visitation at Paray was not the only one to propose public worship of the Sacred shortly before her, had already promoted it. But the Holy See was not content simply to approve these initiatives by establishing a universal feast of the Sacred Heart, and giving the honors of sainthood to John Eudes and Margaret Mary, as well as beatifying Claude La Colombière, the latter's principal counselor. It transformed what had been a private devotion dear to many renowned mystics, including St. Gertrude, the thirteenth-century German Benedictine nun, into an official devotion, indeed one of the deepest and most eloquent in the Catholic tradition.

We can readily see that this devotion follows the most authentic Gospel teaching when we remember that the heart, in every human language, is considered the image and symbol of love. Devotion to the Sacred Heart, therefore, can only be devotion to the created and uncreated love of Christ, insofar as it deigned to beat in a heart of flesh and blood, a human heart. To go to the heart of Jesus is to go to the wellspring of our salvation. Could anything be closer to the Gospel?

As the present study unfolds, we shall have more to say about this primary idea of devotion to the Sacred Heart, following the lessons of St. Margaret Mary, or more truly, of her heavenly Visitor. Unless we are gravely mistaken, what we shall say will throw light on the essential idea of the Mystical Body of Christ. Let us point out right away that the idea of *reparation,* which is at the core of devotion to the Sacred Heart, implies a deep solidarity among all members of the Mystical Body, a solidarity so all-embracing that everything the saints do in the Church, in union with Jesus Christ their Model and Master, compensates before God for the offenses of sinners and obtains for them the graces of conversion and salvation.

But all this will be made clear in the simple account we are about to give, one of many, about Margaret Mary and the promises which were made to the world through her by our Lord Jesus Christ.

1

Family—Childhood—Education

FAMILY

Margaret Mary Alacoque was born on the feast of St. Mary Magdalene, July 22, 1647, in the diocese of Autun, France. Her father, Claude Alacoque, was a royal notary at Vérosvres, and also performed the functions of judge in several of the seigneurial jurisdictions that the French Revolution would later abolish. In the mid-seventeenth century the royal court had merely reduced their scope. They were the seigneuries of Le Terreau, La Roche, Corcheval, and Le Pressy. His residence was in the hamlet of Les Janots or Le Terreau, which was part of the village of Lautecour, a dependency of Vérosvres.

It is certain he was considered a very important man in that region of France.

Monsieur Alacoque already had four children, three sons and a daughter, when the predestined apostle of the Sacred Heart was born to him. She, in turn, was followed by another daughter and son, bringing the total of the Alacoque children to seven.

On July 24th, two days after her birth, the child was baptized and given the one name of *Marguerite*. It was not until she was confirmed that she took the additional name of *Marie*. As it happened, due to untoward circumstances, Margaret Mary Alacoque was not confirmed until 1669, when she was 22 years old. Her godfather was Anthony Alacoque, her father's first cousin and pastor of Vérosvres, and her godmother was a noble lady, wife of the Lord of Corcheval, Claude de Fautrières, née Marguerite de Saint-Amour. Hence the name of Marguerite given the infant. It is an indication of the high esteem in which the Alacoque family was held in that region that a noble lady of the area was willing to become Margaret Mary's godmother, and later on to receive her into her home.

Margaret Mary grew up in a wholesome and profoundly Christian environment. Her earliest childhood memories are proof of this. There is nothing of greater import for a human being than this first mysterious awakening of the soul. But this very awakening depends inevitably on the milieu in which it takes place, above all on the tenor of family life.

Here is what our saint wrote between the years 1686 and 1687, in obedience to her spiritual director, Father Rolin, concerning her childhood:

"O my only Love! How indebted I am to You for having predisposed me from my earliest childhood, by becoming the Master and Possessor of my heart, although You well knew how it would resist You! As soon as I could know myself, You made my soul see the ugliness of sin, and impressed such horror of sin upon my heart, that the slightest stain caused me unbearable torment; and to put a stop to my childish impetuousness one needed only to tell me it was offending God. This stopped me short, and kept me from doing whatever I was eager to do."

"It is good for a man to bear the yoke from his youth," Jeremiah the Prophet tells us (Lamentations 3:27).

Providential dispositions must somehow be present within man's fallen nature for a very young child to be formed and as though molded by ideas that are still totally beyond his comprehension. Indeed, what did little Margaret know of God, of His supreme authority, of man's duty to obey Him? And above all, what could she know of sin, of its nature, its ugliness, its poisoned fruits? Obviously, very little.

But it sufficed for someone to talk to her of God, to tell her that we must love and obey Him in all things, and fear offending Him, to fill her completely with the thought of God. Her earliest education, that is to say, the first victories within her of good over evil, of God over Satan, was entirely founded on the Christian faith. And this explains what she went on to say in the story of her early life:

"Without knowing what it was, I continually felt the need to say these words: 'O my God, I consecrate my purity to You and I make a vow of perpetual chastity to You.' Once I said these words between the two elevations of the holy Mass, which I usually attended on my bare knees, however cold it might be. I did not understand what I had done, or what the word 'vow' meant either, any more than what chastity meant. My one desire was to hide in some forest, and the only thing that held me back was the fear of finding people there."

How old was she when she made a vow of virginity without knowing what this vow meant? Probably four or five years of age at the most. However, she would never forget it. We shall see that this vow, pronounced at an extremely early age, would later have a decisive influence on the course of her life.

To understand these things, we would have to know the conversations she heard and took part in at home, what admonitions were given to very small children, what gestures they were taught to make with their hands when they addressed Jesus, what stories from the *Lives of the Saints* delighted the imagination of these young minds. Evidently, each child reacts to such things in his own individual and personal way. It is interesting to note, however, that of the three children who survived among the seven born to the Alacoque family, only one married and had children, Chrysostom Alacoque. Margaret, the next after him, became a nun, and the youngest son became a priest.

God, hatred of sin, purity, chastity, vows made to the Lord, attendance at Mass, "kneeling on bare knees," the desire to go out into the woods alone and pray—these were the first fruits of Margaret's education in the Christian religion. And here we find in essence her entire life of reparation of later years!

AT CORCHEVAL

Such early religious training was already the grace of graces. But it would be silly to think this was wholly a matter of human influences, of unconscious reactions to the pressures of a tradition and a milieu. It can be said our destinies are written out in advance in the sense that God is concerned with each of His children. Obviously, He makes His own mysterious choices, foreseen from all eternity. He prepares "vocations" according to His plans long before they become apparent to anyone, even those whom He has chosen. Margaret Mary came to understand this, as we can see from quotations from her *Autobiography.* She attributed everything to this "one Love that had predisposed her from earliest childhood," and that had become "the Master and Owner of her heart."

If her first vow of virginity was made when she was four or five years old, it is probable she made it at the château of Corcheval. Her godmother, Madame de Fautrières, had asked her parents to let her live with her. Margaret stayed at the château for long periods of time between her fourth and her eighth years. As was the custom among the nobility, she was entrusted to the care of trustworthy women, specifically charged with instructing her in matters of religion. Of these two women, one was cheerful and indulgent, the other gloomy and severe. It would have been quite natural for Margaret to take a greater liking to the former. But such was not the case. Even during these tender years—and this was a sign of God's action within her—it seemed as though she always went against the inclinations of her nature.

It seems it was later learned that the first of the women, the one who seemed so prepossessing, was of questionable character. It is probable that the less gracious woman spoke more truly of God and of His saints. And this is presumably why the child, contrary to the tendencies natural to her age, always preferred the woman who rebuffed her to the one who treated her more gently. There was a chapel in the château, where the Blessed Sacrament was reserved. Margaret's greatest delight was to kneel before the tabernacle, unless perhaps it was to saunter in a neighboring wood.

In 1654, when Margaret was seven, her godmother lost her husband. As the lady remarried in 1656, it is generally thought the child returned to her mother's home in 1655. During that year, Margaret also lost her father, who died at the age of forty-one, leaving a rather tangled inheritance.

AT BOARDING SCHOOL

Margaret's two older brothers were sent to a boarding school at Cluny run by the Benedictines. These were John and Claude Philibert. The latter became a lawyer and died on September 25, 1665. John, the eldest child of the family, died at the age of twenty-three in 1663.

Their mother, whose maiden name was Philiberte Lamyn, found herself in a very precarious situation as the result of her husband's death. The house she lived in was owned jointly by her husband and her brother-in-law, Toussaint Delaroche. It was the latter who took over the management of the entire property, and practically reduced Madame Alacoque's role to that of a household servant.

Meanwhile, Margaret was sent as a boarder to the school of the Urbanist Poor Clares of Charolles, to complete her education. These nuns were a branch of the Second Order of St. Francis, and were named in honor of Pope Urban IV (1261-1264), who instituted the feast of *Corpus Christi.* Although they had mitigated the primitive Franciscan Rule, they still led a very austere life. It was while a student with these sisters that Margaret was admitted to her First Communion at the age of nine, which was then considered very young.

Here again, we can discern a special grace at work. There is nothing harder to understand, especially for children, than the cross, the spirit of penance, avoidance of even innocent pleasure. Now, Margaret's First Communion initiated her into this mystery of mysteries. "The folly of the cross" was something she quickly understood as though by instinct. Surely, she could not have explained the theory of it. She was not a theologian and had not read St. Paul. But her divine Master guided her. And we can see clearly that He was preparing her long in advance for the mission that was to be hers in the history of the Church.

Here is what she says about it in her *Autobiography:*

"I was placed in a religious house where I was admitted to Communion when I was about nine years old, and this Communion made all these little pleasures and amusements so bitter to me that I could not enjoy any of them, even though I sought them eagerly. But when I wanted to engage in some of them with my companions, I always felt something that drew me away and called me into some little corner, and giving me no rest until I had complied. And then, it would make me pray, but almost always prostrate, or on my bare knees, or making genuflections, providing no one saw me. But it caused me strange torment when someone saw me."

Besides, the religious life as Margaret saw her teachers practice it held a strong fascination for her. As she herself has said:

"I was very eager to do everything I saw the nuns do, as I considered them all to be saints and thought that if I were a nun I would become a saint too. My desire for this way of life grew so strong that I lived only for it, although I didn't think they were sufficiently withdrawn from the world to suit me. But as I knew of no others, I thought I would have to remain there."

There is no mention in the above passage of her vow of virginity. She would speak of it later. But she had already come to think that somehow this vow demanded life in a convent. In any case, she knew she wanted to be a saint. The nuns, as her childish eyes saw them, were all saints. Therefore she would be a nun, too. Her child's logic was correct. And yet she had a vague notion of a life more withdrawn from the world than the one she saw the Urbanist Poor Clares living at Charolles.

ILLNESS

Margaret might have remained at Charolles had she not been obliged to return home because of illness. When she was about eleven years old, she suffered a serious attack of rheumatism which kept her bedridden for four years. She has described it for us:

"...I was stricken with such a pitiful sickness that I was unable to walk for about four years. My bones were coming through the skin everywhere, and this is the reason why I was left in this convent only two years, and no remedy for my illness was found except to dedicate me to the Blessed Virgin, promising her that if she cured me I would some day be one of her daughters. As soon as I made this vow I was cured, with a new protection from the most Blessed Virgin, who now became so completely the mistress of my heart that she looked upon me as belonging to her and governed me as being dedicated to her, reproving me for my faults, and teaching me to do the will of my God. And once when I had sat down to say our rosary, she stood before me and gave me this reprimand that has never been erased from my mind, although I was then very young: 'My daughter, I'm surprised that you serve me so negligently!' These words made such an impression on my soul that they have served me all my life."

In order to understand this last passage, we must realize that Margaret had a very great devotion to the Blessed Virgin Mary. It certainly had come to her from her mother and from her home training. The Virgin Mary had always been presented to her as the mediatrix and advocate through whom the Christian can approach the divine Master without fear. She has written in her *Autobiography:*

"The most Blessed Virgin Mary has always taken the greatest care of me, who turned to her in all my needs, and she has saved me from very great dangers. I didn't dare address myself to her divine Son at all, but always to her, to whom I offered the little crown of the rosary [five decades of the rosary] kneeling on my bare knees, or genuflecting and kissing the ground each time I said a '*Hail Mary.*'"

It seemed a kind of negligence for her to sit comfortably while saying her rosary, and our Blessed Lady reprimanded her for it, as we have seen. She would never forget it. She was called to a very special mission, and she was being prepared for it by the unusual demands made upon her.

Margaret belonged to that group of persons from whom God demands a great deal because He gives them much and expects great things of them. The Gospel warns us that he who has received five talents will be judged on five talents, and he who has received only two or even one will be judged by what he has done with his talent or talents. But the same passage of Scripture also says that he who does not use his talents to make them bear fruit will have them taken away, and they will be given to those who have the most (see Matthew 25:14-30). Can we perhaps deduce from this that the graces wasted by sinners are given to the great saints? For to the saints devolves the great and mysterious task of making reparation and compensation for others. This is what we shall discover in the life of Margaret Mary Alacoque.

MARGARET ALMOST FORGETS HER PROMISE

However, let no one imagine that Margaret's road to sanctity was straight and free of detours. She has admitted she was tempted at times to abandon the path of perfection.

As we have said, she was about eleven years old when she was stricken with the serious illness that lasted four years. Then, in 1662 the Blessed Virgin Mary restored her to health and she vowed some day to become one of her daughters. To her mind and her mother's no doubt, this could only mean she would enter the religious life, and probably the Order of the Visitation, because these nuns were usually called "Daughters of Saint Mary."

Nine years were to elapse before Margaret Mary asked admittance to the Visitation monastery at Paray-le-Monial. Nine years is a long time for a young girl who has made such a vow! What happened to her inwardly and in her outward life in the interval?

These nine years can be divided into three periods. During the first period, Margaret tended to enjoy her return to health, without thinking very much about her vow, but she and her mother were subjected to painful humiliations. In the second, her family's great concern was to marry her off, and the humiliations from her close relatives ceased. Finally, in the third period, her vocation made itself felt again, and she decided to enter a convent. We shall discuss this in the next chapter, but for the present let us look at the first two phases.

HUMILIATIONS

Margaret Mary has clearly described what happened to her after her cure when she was fifteen:

"Having regained my health, I thought only of pleasure and enjoying my freedom, with no concern about carrying out my promise.... As soon as I began to breathe in the air of good health, I turned to vanity and affection for creatures, flattering myself that the tender love my mother and brothers had for me left me free to seek my little pleasures and enjoy myself as much as I wanted...."

This is not to imply that she began to commit serious sins. No, for if that had been the case she would have admitted it, so great was her desire to diminish herself in the eyes of others.

She was feeling better. She was regaining her love of life. It was all very natural. But this return to the natural, this flight from the cross, this love of the comforts of the bourgeois life that could be hers would later appear to her as a betrayal of her divine Spouse. For her whole life was meant to be lived in the shadow of Calvary. Her great fault was to forget the cross. This is no mere conjecture on our part. She has said so in the following commentary:

"O my God! I did not then realize what You have made me know and experience since...that inasmuch as Your Sacred Heart brought me forth on Calvary with so much suffering, the life You gave me there could only be sustained by the food of the cross, which was to become my favorite delicacy."

Later on, at the height of her spiritual development, she would have a supernatural preference for penance, humiliation, opposition, for sufferings of body and soul, to be more closely identified with Jesus crucified. She was certainly far from such heights at this time. She even seemed to be going backward, retrogressing from what she had been in her earlier years. This was the period of her great "*infidelities.*" Indeed, they would have counted as nothing for most other people. But she judged all these things in the light of the intimacy she had attained with the heart of Jesus She probably never read the works of the great mystic, St. John of the Cross. But she could certainly have said as he did: "The whole universe is not worthy of a single thought on man's part, because he owes his whole being to God alone, and every thought we do not direct toward God is stolen from Him!"

If this is indeed true, how many thefts have we not committed in our lives! Margaret would later consider the better part of her life between her fifteenth and twenty-fourth year as stolen from God.

At any rate, during this first phase which lasted from her fifteenth to her eighteenth year, God Himself called her to order, taking away all delight from even her most innocent pleasures.

Home life became a kind of purgatory for her and her mother. As we have seen, after her father's death, close relatives of Madame Alacoque, the Delaroches, had taken over the management of the home and of the family property. The succession remained somewhat controversial. The entire Delaroche family – Toussaint, his wife, his mother-in-law, and even their aged woman servant – came to exercise tyrannical control over Margaret and her mother. They inflicted all sorts of little insults on them. It was a war of pinpricks. When such a war is waged all day, every day, it can be very painful indeed. Margaret Mary has told us something about it:

"My mother had given up her authority in the house, and handed it over to a few others who took advantage of it in such a way that both she and I were in complete captivity. It is not that I want to blame these persons in what I am about to say, or claim they did wrong in making me suffer – my God did not allow me to entertain such a thought – for I want only to consider them as instruments which He was using to carry out His holy will."

How far did this "captivity" go? She has told us:

"And so we had lost all power in the house, and we didn't dare do anything without permission. It was a constant war and everything was under lock and key, so that often I couldn't even find anything to wear to go to holy Mass, unless I borrowed a cape and a dress. It was then I began to feel my captivity, and sank so deep into it that I did nothing and never went out without the assent of three persons."

Where could she turn for help? Margaret was too good a Christian not to know. She turned to God. At this time of her life she still had no idea of the devotion to the Sacred Heart. But she knew that her Jesus was really present on the altar. Devotion to the Blessed Sacrament thus became more precious to her than ever before. But even in this matter, she suffered new humiliations:

"It was at that time that I began to find all my pleasure and consolation in the Most Blessed Sacrament of the altar. But since I was living in a village at some distance from the church, I could go only with the permission of these persons, and it happened that when one was willing, the other did not agree. And often, when I expressed my chagrin with tears I was accused of having made a rendezvous with some boys and of being disappointed because I could not go and meet them, using the pretext that I wanted to go to Mass or to Benediction of the Blessed Sacrament. And I who felt such horror of these things in my heart that I would have preferred to see my body torn into a thousand pieces than to entertain such a thought!..."

Such suspicions about her filled her with unspeakable desolation. But even this kindled great yearnings in her heart. Rebuffed, calumniated, forcefully confined to the house, how did she pass the time? She tells us:

"That is why, not knowing where to seek refuge except in some corner of the garden or stable or some other secret place, where I was able to get on my knees to pour out my heart, through my tears, before my God, through the intercession of my good Mother, in whom I had put all my trust, I would stay there for entire days, without drinking or eating anything...."

Let us try to picture these years of misery. For a girl between fifteen and eighteen, it should have been a time of beautiful dreams, of quiet and fervent study, the age when everyone lavishes little favors and attentions on the burgeoning flower. For Margaret, this was the age of tears, the age of persecutions and deprivations. She has admitted that "sometimes some of the poor folk from the village would give me a little milk or fruit in the evening, out of compassion for me."

We need not be too surprised that Margaret's long absences from the house, her solitary retreats in prayer and tears, her turning to the peasants of the area to obtain a little food, brought new insults from her family.

"And when I returned home, it was with such great fear and trembling that I felt like a poor criminal who was coming to be convicted and sentenced, and I would have considered myself more fortunate to go and beg for my bread than to live like that, for very often I didn't dare take any food at table. For, from the moment I entered the house, the attack started over again more furiously than before: about my not having done the housework and taken care of the children...and without having a chance to say a single word, I set to work with the servants. After which, I would spend my nights as I had spent the days, weeping before my crucifix...."

THE CRUCIFIX ANSWERS

From the purely human point of view, such things inspire pity. But for Margaret Mary, in the light of what she later came to know, all that happened to her at this time was secretly planned by Providence.

This was the unfolding of her vocation. The divine Crucified told her so:

"[He] explained to me, although I didn't understand, that He wanted to become the absolute Master of my heart and make me conform in every way with His life of suffering, that this was why He wanted to become my Master, by making Himself present to my soul, to make me act as He had acted amid His cruel sufferings, which He made me see He had endured through love."

Through these persecutions, Margaret thus made great progress in understanding the cross, even though she didn't realize it at the time. She came to love her pain! The Crucified pursued her relentlessly. Now she wanted only to love her persecutors, even for their cruelties.

Let us allow her to explain herself:

"And from that moment on, my soul was so completely penetrated with Him that I would have wished my sufferings had not ceased for an instant. For He was always present to me, in the form of a crucifix or of an *Ecce homo* carrying His cross, and this implanted into me so much compassion and love for His sufferings that all my sufferings became light in comparison with the yearning I had to suffer, to conform with my suffering Jesus. And I regretted that the hands sometimes raised to strike me were held back and did not unleash all their harshness against me...."

We must look more closely into the meaning of these lines. They reveal a Margaret Mary already reaching the heights where she would spend the rest of her life. *She had learned the cross!* This was a very great thing! She now had the suffering Jesus constantly before her eyes, but a Jesus who was asking her to suffer with Him, who wanted her to share His own anguish. She would certainly make far greater progress in this path of perfection, but it would always remain the same path. Her entire *Autobiography* is proof of it. Jesus Crucified had conquered her soul. He would never let her go. And just as it was His practice to pray for His persecutors, to make satisfaction and reparation for the sinners that we all are, so Margaret Mary learned through Him to pray for her persecutors.

"I felt incessantly impelled to render all sorts of services and to do kind deeds for these true friends of my soul,[1] and I would gladly have sacrificed myself for them, since I had no greater delight than to do good to them and to say all the good about them that I could...."

However, as she wrote these lines she was careful to point out that all the merit of this charity, that Jesus Himself commanded her to reveal in obedience, came from Him alone.

"He had taken possession of my will and would not allow me even to formulate any complaint, any murmur, or resentment against these persons or even permit anyone to pity me or have compassion on me."

To complete the picture of this period, we should note that her heaviest cross was her inability to lighten those her mother was enduring. She had made it a rule never to talk to her mother about them, for fear of offending God by failing in charity or patience. But it caused her deep inner suffering to see her mother reduced to a kind of slavery in her own home.

Margaret's concern was aggravated when her mother suffered an attack of "deadly erysipelas" on her face "of frightening extent, redness, and hardness." And Madame Alacoque was very inadequately treated for this illness. No one in the house paid any attention to her. Margaret was the only one to take care of her beloved patient, and she had no one to help, no knowledge, and no medications. Her only

1. If we rightly understand this passage and those that complement it, the persecutions at home came to her from three women: her aunt Delaroche, her grandmother Alacoque, and the old servant woman. Mr. Toussaint Delaroche, her uncle, was an unpolished but well-meaning man, and must have been above all these bickerings.

recourse was to her "ordinary refuge," the most Blessed Virgin Mary. In fact she prayed so well, especially on one New Year's day when she was able to go to Mass, that on returning home she found the boil had burst. Her mother's cheek had opened and pus was pouring out of it. Not knowing what she should do, she bandaged her mother's face as well as she could, overcoming her natural revulsions.

Here again, she experienced help from her Jesus:

"I felt so much courage and trust in the kindness of my Lord who seemed always to be present, that she finally was completely cured in a few days, against all human expectations."

MENTAL PRAYER

One of the things Margaret has carefully recorded about this period of her life is the way she learned mental prayer. Prayer and contemplation, which assumed such importance in her life, are such an integral part of the Christian's ascent toward sanctity that we should pay close attention to what she has to say on the subject.

First of all, mystical theologians tell us that there are two sorts of mental prayer—*active* prayer and *passive* prayer, the latter including several ascending degrees of contemplation. In active prayer, man seems to make most of the effort, under the impulsion of grace. In passive prayer, divine grace takes all the initiative and more or less governs the human will.

The ordinary process is to begin with active prayer. Then passive prayer comes later as a reward and gift of love from God Himself.

The truth is that the moment God makes Himself present to us and we live in this presence, there is *mental prayer.* But let us listen to Margaret Mary:

"Through this time of illness, I almost never laid down or slept and took almost no food. But my divine Master would console me and sustain me with perfect conformity to His most holy will, and I attributed to Him alone everything that happened to me, saying: 'O my sovereign Master! It would not happen unless You wanted it to! But I thank You for allowing it, so as to make me conform to You.'"

There can be little doubt that Margaret was initiated into mental prayer by Jesus in person, and the fruit of it was her wonderful acceptance of all that happened to her. In view of what we have said about passive prayer, it was to be expected that Jesus should lead her at once into passive prayer. Let us read with even greater care as she explains:

"In the midst of all this, I felt so strongly drawn to mental prayer that it caused me great suffering not to know or to be able to learn how to practice it, as I had no conversations with spiritual persons. And all I knew were these words, 'mental prayer,' that ravished my heart."

As we know, this word was in the air at the time. All the books of piety spoke of nothing but mental prayer and its methods. It was quite common for devout persons to ask each other to what degree of mental prayer they had ascended.

This topic of conversation was considered much more interesting than politics or the weather. Margaret had therefore heard of mental prayer. The word held an unknown but exquisite savor for her. But she knew nothing more about it.

As always, she asked her Jesus to instruct her:

"And having addressed myself to my sovereign Master, He taught me how He wanted me to practice it, and this has served me throughout my life. He made me humbly prostrate myself before Him, to ask His forgiveness for everything I had done to offend Him. And after adoring Him, I offered Him my mental prayer without knowing how I should go about it. Then He presented Himself in the mystery in which He wanted me to meditate upon Him and He made my mind concentrate so well on it, keeping my soul and all my powers engulfed within Himself, that I was not aware of distractions, but my heart felt consumed with the desire to love Him, and this gave me an insatiable desire for Holy Communion and for suffering."[1]

Obviously, Margaret was learning mental prayer from Jesus Himself, but she didn't realize what was happening.

"Although this pursuit was more delightful to me than I can express, I didn't realize it was mental prayer and I felt continually persecuted to engage in mental prayer, promising Him that as soon as He taught it to me, I would spend as much time as I could in mental prayer...."

And so she continued to implore her Jesus: "Teach me mental prayer, O sweet Master!" But Jesus probably just smiled from heaven. She promised to devote all possible time to mental prayer, and she was already doing it, without realizing it.

"Nevertheless, His goodness kept me so completely engrossed in the pursuit I have just described—mental prayer, in short—that it gave me a distaste for vocal prayers, which I could not say before the Blessed Sacrament, where I felt so completely engrossed that I was never bored. And I would have spent entire days and nights there, without drinking or eating, and without knowing what I was doing, except that I was consumed in His presence like a burning candle, to return Him love for love. And I couldn't stay in the back of the church. No matter how embarrassed I felt, I would go as close as I possibly could to the most Blessed Sacrament. I considered myself fortunate and envied only those who could receive Communion often and who were free to remain before the most Blessed Sacrament...."

This extraordinary devotion to the Blessed Sacrament and to frequent Communion—which was a far

1. In this text we used the word "consumed" instead of "consummated." The saint always said *consummate* when she meant *consume*.

cry from the Jansenistic spirit then raging in France—once played a very strange trick on her. The pastor of the parish had said in his sermon before Christmas that those who had not taken a nap before Midnight Mass were not to receive Communion. What did he mean by that? Perhaps he hoped to keep his parishioners from dozing off at Midnight Mass. In any event, Margaret obeyed by lying down, but she had been unable to sleep because of her great joy and her anticipation of receiving Communion. Since she had not napped, she didn't dare receive Communion out of fear of disobeying her pastor! And so she spent Christmas, the great day of rejoicing, in tears, "which," she said, "served as my food and pleasure."

WORLDLY VANITIES

And now came the phase of her greatest worldliness. She was eighteen. There was question of marrying her. In her region she was considered a good match, and soon she was faced with the serious problem of fidelity to her vow of virginity. Was this vow valid? Had she really understood what she was doing when she made it? Did this vow obligate her in conscience? Those around her didn't have a moment's hesitation. Her own mother, who must certainly have known about it, was counting on her daughter's marriage to escape the humiliating and painful servitude in which she had lived since her husband's death, and this had been over ten years.

In a very short time, everything seems to have changed at home. Margaret's aunt and grandmother, and even the old woman servant, now wanted her elegantly attired and to appear as much as possible in society. She has described this transformation in her home situation:

"The devil got several excellent suitors in the eyes of the world to seek me out, to make me break the vow I had made. That attracted a great deal of company that I had to receive, which was a real agony for me. For on the one hand my relatives were pressing me in that direction, especially my mother who was constantly weeping and telling me that I was her only hope of escaping her misery, because of the consolation she would have living with me as soon as I was well established in the world."

A heart-rending battle broke loose within her, which she has described:

"God was pursuing my heart so eagerly that He gave me no truce; for my vow was always before my eyes, knowing that if I should break it I would suffer terrible punishment. The devil played on my love and devotion for my mother, constantly showing me the tears she was shedding, and if I were to become a nun I would cause her to die of sorrow and I would answer for it before God, for she was totally dedicated to my care and service. This caused me unbearable torment, for I loved her tenderly, and she me, to the point that we couldn't live without seeing each other."

Meanwhile, Margaret, in obedience to her family's wishes, began to attend social functions and to wear elegant clothes. She claims she even tried "to have as much pleasure as she could."

It was probably during this period that she committed what she considered to be the greatest sin of her whole life. She says: "Once during the carnival time, I was with other young girls and wore a masquerade costume out of a desire to please, and this has been a cause of sorrow and tears all my life, as well as the sin I committed by putting on this garb of vanity, out of the same motive of pleasing the persons cited above...."

It was in reference to this "crime" that she once wrote:

"But I had committed great crimes, too!"

The saints have such scruples. In order to understand them, we must also keep before our eyes the graces which God has bestowed upon them and the great things He expects of them.

2

The Religious Vocation

THE GREAT STRUGGLES

It seems that Margaret's great struggles continued from her eighteenth to her twenty-fourth year. This does not mean she waited until she was twenty-four to make her decision. Even after she had made up her mind, the struggles continued until she entered the convent.

Every time she yielded to her family's wishes by agreeing to take part in social activities and wear lovely gowns in keeping with her condition, she would hear a voice in her heart which spoke more sternly as time went on. Here are some of her confessions on the matter:

"But You, my God, the only witness to the length and breadth of this terrible battle that raged within me and in which I would have succumbed a thousand times without the extraordinary support of Your merciful goodness which had far different plans than those I entertained in my heart—You made me know in this encounter, as well as in many others, that it would be very hard and difficult to resist this powerful goad of Your love, although my malice and infidelity made me use all my strength and efforts to resist it and quench its action within me...."

Margaret related her secret struggles at great length. Such combats occur so often with varying degrees of violence in the course of religious vocations that it is of great interest to cite the following page from our saint's pen.

She was trying to evade the urgent calls of her sovereign Master. Nature had not yet been overcome; the world still exerted a powerful attraction upon her. She was anxious to please her mother. Arguments were not lacking to make her believe it was her duty to comply with her family's wishes.

"But all in vain, for in the midst of company and amusement, He [Jesus] shot such burning arrows at me that they completely pierced and consumed my heart. And the pain I experienced stupefied me. And that was still not enough for a heart as ungrateful as mine to make it surrender. I felt as though I had been bound and was being dragged by force of ropes so that at last I was obliged to follow the one who was calling me to some secret place. And He reprimanded me severely, for He was jealous of my miserable heart which was enduring frightful persecutions...."

Countless other young girls, in love with Divine Love, have passed through similar torments. It is through such battles that generous souls reveal their worth.

When Margaret was alone with her Lord, she felt as though utterly overwhelmed.

"And after asking His forgiveness, my face against the ground, He made me take a long and harsh discipline. And then I would return, just as before, to my resistances and vanities. And at night, when I took off those cursed liveries of Satan, I mean those vain adornments, the instruments of his malice, my sovereign Master would appear to me, as He was in His scourging, all disfigured, reprimanding me in a strange way: that my vanity had reduced Him to this state—and that I was losing such precious time for which He would require a strict account at the hour of death; that I was betraying and persecuting Him, after which He gave me so many proofs of His love and of His desire that I conform to Him! All this penetrated me so forcefully and made such painful wounds in my heart that I wept bitterly and it would be hard for me to express all that I suffered and what was going on within me."

SEVERE PENANCES

Margaret Mary's inner struggles against herself and against her true vocation could have ended in sterile sentiments. She could have allowed her life to pass in an unending struggle between opposing desires, like the pendulum of a clock swinging to and fro. How often do great upsurges of soul plummet to earth and die! But with Margaret, sentiment and emotion were instantly translated into action.

Jesus reprimanded her. He appeared to her in His scourging. Without knowing it, she was engaging in mental prayer as she contemplated Him in His mysterious sufferings. He was calling her to share in His sufferings, which, she knew, had ransomed the world. Jesus Himself was initiating her into the spiritual life by making her understand that all spirituality is a sharing in His own life, which is the source of all grace and holiness.

What did Jesus say to her and how was He preparing her for her future mission? We find the answer on the very next page of her *Autobiography:*

"Not knowing what the spiritual life was, since I had never been instructed in it or heard speak of it, I knew only what my Master taught me and made me do with His loving violence. In order to avenge myself in some way against myself for the wrongs I was doing Him and to regain this likeness and conformity to Him, to relieve the pain that oppressed me, I would bind this miserable, criminal body with knotted ropes, which I tied so tightly that it could scarcely breathe and eat. I left these ropes around me so long that they sank so deep into the flesh, and it grew over them, so that I could pull them off only with great violence and cruel pain. And likewise for the little chains that I bound tightly around my arms, which pulled off pieces of flesh when they were removed. And besides I slept on a board, or on sticks with pointed knots, which I used as my bed. And then too I took the discipline, striving to find some remedy for my combats and for the sufferings I endured within me, in comparison with which everything I could suffer on the outside—even though the humiliations and contradictions I have spoken of earlier continued unabated and tended to increase rather than diminish—all these things, I say, seemed only a kind of refreshment compared to my interior sufferings, which I did myself so much violence to bear in silence and keep hidden, as my good Master taught me, that there was no external evidence of them, except that people saw me grow pale and parched...."

Amid all these struggles, she didn't even have the consolation of feeling she was at peace with her God and not offending Him. Quite the contrary. She was constantly racked with regrets and remorse. Worse by far, she thought she was doomed to hell.

We have seen that she labeled as "*crimes*" infidelities that would seem very trivial to most girls of her age. It can certainly be said that her ultrasensitive soul magnified into sins mere scruples or passing thoughts in which there was no sin on her part. This did not prevent her from being constantly tormented by them, through the permission of God. St. Augustine had written long before: "*Our souls are restless, O God, until they rest in You!*" It is in this light that we must understand the following lines Margaret Mary wrote:

"The fears I felt of offending my God tormented me even more than all the rest, for it seemed to me that I was continually sinning, and my sins seemed so serious to me that I was surprised hell did not open up under my feet to swallow up such a miserable sinner. I would have liked to go to confession every day, and yet I could do so only rarely. I esteemed as saints those who were not like me, who could not confess my sins. This caused me many tears."

THE DECISION

And yet, little by little, a resolve was taking form in her heart that would win the day. Her religious vocation was no mere improvisation. She has stated explicitly that she "spent several years amid these torments and struggles and many other sufferings." We have historical evidence to support her claim. Perhaps we should set the date of her Confirmation—the sacrament of fortitude—as the moment when her hesitations came to an end.

We have already mentioned that Margaret was not confirmed until she was twenty-two years old. This was to be brought up against her as an argument against her beatification. But it is certain the delay was through no fault on her part. At that time, it was not rare for a bishop to be away from his official residence for considerable periods of time and fail to administer the sacrament of Confirmation to his flock.

Margaret Mary belonged to the diocese of Autun. The Ordinary of the diocese, Bishop Gabriel de Roquette, was also the king's official chaplain. He took advantage of this title to live at the royal court. It was the neighboring bishop of Châlon-sur-Saône, John de Maupou, who made the diocesan visit during which Margaret was confirmed. She took the name of Marie, which would afterwards be inseparable from her baptismal name. This occurred sometime between August and September, 1669. It was only after this date that she could rightly be called Margaret Mary.

In any event, it was at or around this date that she made her great decision. She would become a nun. It is even probable she had resolved upon it somewhat earlier, but her memory for dates seems to have been blurred. It is not always easy to establish the exact chronology of her life.

We know she spent "several years amid these sufferings and struggles." Since these trials began when she was eighteen, they could not have ended until after her twentieth birthday. Besides, she has said that after she decided to enter the religious life, it was not to be realized for over four or five years. This would bring us far beyond the day in 1671, when we know she knocked at the door of the Monastery of the Visitation at Paray-le-Monial.

Let us simply say that Margaret Mary's great struggles continued from about 1665 to 1668, that she made her resolution in 1668, but reinforced it the following year through the powerful grace of the sacrament of Confirmation, and finally was able to execute her great plan in 1671.

THE BEAUTY OF HER VOCATION

It was very clear in Margaret Mary's memory that her decision was inspired by a change in her divine Master's mode of instructing her:

"For His behavior toward me changed greatly, and He showed me the beauty of the virtues, especially of the three vows of poverty, chastity, and obedience, and told me that in practicing them one becomes a saint. And He told me this because when I prayed to Him I asked Him to make me a saint. And as I read practically no books except the *Lives of the Saints*, I used to say to myself when I opened the book: I must choose one that is very easy to imitate, so I can act the way she did, and become a saint like her."

In reading this passage, we question not her veracity but what she understood by the word "easy." We have already seen her inflict penances on herself that ordinary mortals like us would consider terrifying—those cords digging into her flesh, those little chains biting into her arms, those cruel disciplines, her painful sleeping arrangements. There can be no doubt she drew the ideas for all these austerities from the *Lives of the Saints.*

The fact remains that she wanted to be a saint. She asked her God to help her become one, and God gave her His answer. It is interesting that she received from Him admirable advice to moderate her harshness toward her body. That's a valuable lesson that everyone should take carefully to heart.

"What desolated me was to see that I offended my God so much. And I thought that the saints had not offended Him as I had, or at least if a few of them had done so they had spent the rest of their lives doing penance, and this made me very eager to do penance, too. But my divine Master instilled in me such a great fear of following my own will that, despite everything I could do, He would agree to it only when I did it through love and under obedience...."

Thank goodness! Such austerities, without spiritual guidance, could be dangerous. Jesus made her see this, and she stopped them. She realized now that Christ asks for our love first and above all! But this love must be translated into action.

"This filled me with great desires to love Him and to accomplish all my actions through obedience. I didn't know how to practice either one, and I thought it was a crime to say I loved God, because I saw my works belied my words. I asked Him to teach me what He wanted me to do, in order to please and love Him...."

At this period of her life, Jesus was her only teacher. She looked to Him alone for guidance. And her trust was rewarded. Jesus had taught her how to practice mental prayer; He had dissuaded her from excessive mortifications unless practiced under obedience. He now taught her how He wanted her to love Him.

She had certainly read in the Gospels the deeply moving words of our Savior: "I assure you, as often as you did it for one of my least brothers, you did it for me" (Matthew 25:40). She remembered the page of Scripture that gave the terrifying picture of the last judgment, in which Jesus identified Himself with the unfortunate, with those who hunger and thirst, who are in prison or suffering illness.

In her eagerness to proceed to action and not merely utter words of love, she felt impelled to seek her Jesus in those around her, in her sick and destitute neighbors.

"He gave me such tender love for the poor that I wanted to converse with no one but them, and He implanted such tender compassion within me for their miseries that, had it been in my power, I would not have kept anything for myself. And when I had money, I gave it to poor children, to encourage them to come to me, so they would learn their catechism and how to pray to God."

This program naturally encountered opposition. At home, Margaret Mary's poor children were considered a nuisance, and it was feared they would soil the lovely furnishings when they were allowed into the house during the cold weather. Reproaches and recriminations rained on Margaret Mary's head. As always, she could do nothing without permission, and whenever she asked her relatives to let the children come, they made a scene.

"All these permissions I was continually asking brought me great rebuffs and captivity."

About this time, she began to "subject" herself inwardly to those with whom she lived, and she found this "a continual torture." Why did she do it? In order to try living the religious life right there at home.

"But I thought I had to subject myself to all those for whom I felt the greatest repugnance, and obey them, to try to see if I could be a nun." The experiment was decisive:

"For this gave them such great authority over me that no nun could have been more captive. But my burning desire to love God made me overcome all difficulties and attentive to do everything most contrary to my inclinations and against which I felt the greatest repugnance. And I felt so strongly impelled to do this that I confessed it when I had failed to follow these inspirations."

If *heroic virtue* consists in making continual efforts to overcome nature, it is clear that even at that time Margaret Mary was practicing love of God in a heroic degree, which is the principal mark of holiness.

This heroism found expression not only in her love for the poor, in her generosity to them, in the lavishness of her material and spiritual alms, but in other ways as well.

OTHER MORTIFICATIONS

At this time, Margaret Mary's mortifications were especially of two sorts. First, in the care she gave to those suffering from painful and revolting sores:

"I felt an extreme revulsion at the sight of these sores. I first had to set about dressing and kissing them in order to conquer myself. But my divine Master supplemented all my ignorance so well, that they were healed in a short time with no other medications than those of Providence, even though these sores were very dangerous. But I had greater confidence in His mercy than in external remedies."

We can readily believe that her gentleness, her charity, the trust she inspired in her patients were far more reliable and effective remedies than the pharmaceutical products then in use.

After long hours of caring for the sick, she might have sought relaxation in innocent amusements suitable to her age and condition. But in this, too, her Jesus pursued her with His holy demands.

"I was naturally inclined to love pleasure and recreation. I couldn't enjoy such things, although I often tried to."

Let us note her words carefully. They show that Margaret Mary was indeed like the rest of us. She loved pleasure and fun. But what happened to her when she sought recreation? She has given us the answer:

"But this sorrowful face that appeared to me, resembling the face of my Savior after His scourging, kept me away from them. For He uttered words of reproach that pierced me to the heart: 'Would you really want this pleasure? And I who never sought any, and endured all sorts of suffering for love of you and to win your heart! And you still want to refuse to give it to me?'

"All this made a great impression on my soul, but I admit in good faith that I didn't understand any of it because my mind was still too earthly and unspiritual."

When she wrote these lines much later, she had finally come to realize that Jesus had been preparing her for the future. For she added:

"It seemed that He had set out to pursue me and continually oppose His goodness to my malice, His love to my ingratitudes, which have been the cause of my greatest sorrow throughout my life."

FIRST INDICATIONS

However, Margaret Mary's relations with her divine Master should not be viewed as a kind of mysterious and enigmatic game. She humbled herself before Him. She asked Him questions. She protested her lowliness, her infidelities, her faults. And this very humility drew down upon her new graces and light.

One day, in answer to her anguished questions, Jesus gave her the following answer which she recorded:

"It is because I want to make you a composite of my love and mercy."

On another occasion:

"I chose you as my spouse and we promised to be faithful to each other when you made your vow of chastity to me. It is I who pressed you to make it before the world had any part of your heart, for I wanted it to be perfectly pure and unsullied by earthly affections. And to keep it that way, I removed all the malice from your will so it could not be corrupted. Then I placed you in the care of my holy Mother, so she might fashion you according to my wishes."

Clearly, her interior life was not stagnant. She was constantly progressing. Her devotion to the Blessed Virgin Mary continued to grow, for she realized this was the path by which she would reach her Jesus.

And so, in the year 1667, four years before she entered the convent, Margaret Mary vowed to fast every Saturday in honor of our Blessed Lady, to recite the Office of the Immaculate Conception (a dogma not yet defined) as soon as she could read Latin, and to recite seven *Hail Mary's* daily while genuflecting, in honor of the Seven Sorrows of Mary.

Here is another remarkable detail. Fifty years before St. Louis Mary Grignion de Montfort, she practiced holy slavery to Mary, which he was to teach. She wrote:

"[I] made myself her slave forever, asking her not to refuse me this role. I used to talk to her simply, like a child to a good Mother for whom I already felt a truly tender love."

SUPREME ATTACK

Although she had decided to become a nun no one around her seemed to believe such a resolve could be final. Doubts even arose in her own heart. Later on, she would attribute these doubts to the devil, whose arguments and objections she has related:

"Satan used to say to me continually: 'Poor wretch, what do you think you are doing, wanting to be a nun? You will be the laughingstock of everybody, because you will never persevere, and how humiliating it will be to give up the religious habit and leave a convent! Where can you hide after that?' "

And then she would burst into tears.

But there were far more serious obstacles. Her mother whom she loved so much kept begging her to give up her plan. Her relatives supported her mother's view on this point. Her two elder brothers had died a few years earlier, and this was an added argument against her vocation. Her mother probably avoided crying in her presence. But, to quote Margaret Mary:

"...She was continually weeping whenever she talked about it to anyone, and they did not fail to come and tell me that I would be the cause of her death if I left her and that I would answer to God for it, for she had no one to serve her, and I could become a nun after her death as well as during her life."

This is also what her brother Chrysostom said. He was then twenty-two and loved his sister very much. He went so far as to offer to increase her dowry from his own resources in order to establish her in society.

All this opposition made a strong impression upon her. Everyone was telling her: "A twenty-year-old girl must get married." She later admitted that one day her resolve to enter the convent was almost shattered. True, she hated the thought of marriage. But when she was approached with the idea of devoting herself to her mother, this touched a responsive chord. She said: *"I began to enter into these sentiments."*

This was the supreme attack. How did she repel it? She has told us about it in her own words.

THE DECISIVE VICTORY

The Blessed Virgin Mary, to whom she owed so much, was the first to come to her rescue. It seems her heavenly Mother reprimanded her severely for her weakness:

"She scolded me severely when she saw me *once again* ready to succumb in the terrible battle that raged within me."[1]

Besides, there was the vow she had made. At moments when she didn't know what she should do, Jesus would remind her of her vow.

"And once after Communion, if I am not mistaken, He made me see that He was the most handsome, the richest, the most powerful, the most perfect and accomplished of lovers, and, since I had been promised to Him for so many years, how was it that I wanted to break everything off with Him, to take up with another: 'Oh! know that if you scorn me in this way, I shall abandon you forever. But if you are faithful to me, I shall not leave you, and I shall become your victory against all my enemies. I forgive your ignorance, because you don't know me yet, but if you are faithful to me and follow me, I will teach you to know me and will manifest myself to you.'"

With all these words reverberating in her ears —Satan's words, the words of the Virgin Mary, Jesus' words—how could she sort out her thoughts and know what truly came from God and what might be delusion? This is the serious problem of the "discernment of spirits." Although Margaret Mary was still quite ignorant of the theory of lofty spirituality, she seems to have come up with the same solution to the problem that the most reliable theologians would have worked out. Here's what she has to say:

1. We have italicized the words "once again," to show that this was not the first time she had felt impelled to renounce the religious life.

"When He [i.e., Jesus] said this to me, He instilled such a great calm within me and my soul felt such great peace, that I determined then and there to die rather than change."

This peace, this profound calm, was for her the sign of God's presence. And the more she strengthened her resolve to become a nun, the more completely this peace possessed her.

"It seemed to me that my bonds were broken and I had nothing more to fear.... Having thus decided in favor of the religious life, this divine Spouse of my soul, lest I escape from Him again, asked me to allow Him to take possession of my freedom, because I was weak. I did not raise any objections, and from that moment He took possession of my freedom so completely that I have not had the use of it since. He penetrated so deep into my heart from that very moment that I renewed my vow, for I was beginning to understand it. I told Him that even if it should cost me a thousand lives, I would never be anything but a nun."

Once she had made her declaration to her Jesus, she no longer hesitated to proclaim it around her. She boldly said she wanted to be a nun, that "all the suitors for her hand would have to be sent away, however advantageous they might be."

THE CHOICE OF A CONVENT

So it was finally agreed. She would become a nun. And yet, according to her own calculations, she was to remain three more years "in the world, amid these struggles." Two things remained to be done before she could accomplish her plans. She had to choose a convent, and she had to obtain the money necessary for her dowry.

Choosing a convent was no easy matter. For Margaret Mary knew only the one where she had been a boarding student as a child, the Urbanist Poor Clares of Charolles. She does not seem to have thought for an instant of joining their community. But one of her uncles had a daughter who was an Ursuline. This was the most flourishing time for this Order. So her uncle put her in contact with his daughter. Naturally, Margaret's cousin did everything she could to encourage her. But it seemed that such a choice would be based on overly human considerations.

"I told her: 'Don't you see that if I enter your convent, it will only be for love of you? I want to go where I shall have neither relative nor acquaintance, so as to be a nun for the love of God.'"

Such an argument was irrefutable. And yet her uncle did not give up. He was Margaret's guardian. He therefore thought he had rights over her as if she were one of his own daughters. He did not allow Margaret's brother Chrysostom to take her back home, much to the latter's disgust. In fact, Chrysostom thought she had agreed with her uncle, and was going to become an Ursuline. He was mistaken. The more Margaret Mary was pressed, the less ready she was to do what was expected of her. In her own words: "A secret voice kept saying to me: 'I don't want you there, but at Saint Mary's.'"

Now, Saint Mary's was the Visitation. Whenever she talked about it, everyone tried to deter her from going there. And yet it was there she felt called to go. It even seemed to her one day that St. Francis de Sales in person, the Founder of the Visitation, was inviting her to enter there and not elsewhere.

"And once, as I was looking at a portrait of the great St. Francis de Sales,[1] he seemed to cast such a loving and fatherly glance at me, and called me his

1. It will be helpful to remember that Francis de Sales, who died on December 28, 1622, had been beatified on December 18, 1661, and canonized on April 19, 1665. There had thus been recent celebrations in his honor. Margaret Mary could not help being deeply moved by them.

daughter, that I have always looked upon him after that as my good Father."

And yet the pressures upon her increased to enter St. Ursula's at Mâcon, where she was then staying with her cousin. She didn't know how to get out of it. In the end she might have decided to enter this convent had she not received news that her brother was ill and her mother was close to death. It was such an excellent opportunity to return home that she saw in it a sign of God's will. She set out at once, traveling all night. When she arrived home, she did not find peace. As it happened, her brother's and mother's illnesses were soon over, but the attacks against her vocation began all over again.

"They pointed out that my mother could not live without me, since my short absence from her had been the cause of her sickness, and that I would answer to God for her death. And since this was being told me by members of the clergy, it caused me severe suffering, because of the great affection I had for her, whom the devil was using to make me believe this would be the cause of my eternal damnation."

But Margaret Mary continued to feel pursued by her Jesus. He gave her no rest, she later said. And she for her part redoubled her penances. She would draw a little blood from her fingers in honor of the blood Christ shed for us. She inflicted severe disciplines on her shoulders, to imitate the divine scourging.

Especially during carnival time, that carry-over from pagan orgies, she fasted on bread and water and gave her own portions of food to the poor. The thought that Christ was being offended by sinners was a torture to her. In her own words:

"I would have wanted to be cut into pieces to make reparation for the outrages sinners were committing against His divine Majesty."

Reparation: this would be the motto of her whole life, her particular mission. And in promoting devotion to the Sacred Heart, she would seek *reparative souls.* Later in this book we shall discuss at greater length this capital point which needs to be explained even to Christians of good will.

However, in her penances, Margaret Mary always feared she might be obeying her own will, especially as everyone around her was continually rebuking her. She would have wanted a spiritual director, to guide her. "Alas! my Lord," she begged, "please give me someone to lead me to You!" And Jesus answered: *"Am I not enough for you? What are you afraid of? Can a child who is loved as much as I love you perish in the arms of an almighty Father?"*

GENERAL CONFESSION

Meanwhile, God sent her unexpected help. In 1670 a Franciscan came to Vérosvres to preach the jubilee of Pope Clement X, who had just become the Sovereign Pontiff. The graces of a jubilee are usually the occasion for many sermons and also for general confessions, during which well-disposed souls make great progress.

So Margaret Mary wanted to make a general confession. In her naïveté and fear of forgetting sins, she used books containing detailed examinations of conscience. She copied everything, including sins she would have been "ashamed to pronounce," as she has said herself. She came to the confessional armed with an impressive list of crimes. The good Father quickly realized with whom he was dealing. He refused to allow her to read the voluminous manuscript she had prepared. Instead, he heard her confession in such a way that he set her conscience completely at peace. She confided to him her desire to be a nun and spoke of her brother's opposition. The priest promised to settle the matter with him.

The Franciscan did indeed have a talk with Margaret's brother. Then, after assuring himself that her decision was final, he felt obliged in conscience to encourage her to become a nun.

But first, there remained to be solved two problems we mentioned earlier: the choice of a convent, and the settlement of the dowry.

Margaret Mary had told her brother she would "prefer to die than change her decision." He therefore ceased his opposition to her vocation and began to help her attain her heart's desire.

SAFELY IN PORT

As we follow the biography of our saint, we can see that few vocations have been as violently opposed and for so long. Without mentioning the first phase between her fifteenth and eighteenth years, she had six long years of incessant struggles before arriving in port. But finally difficulties seemed to abate. The last opposition, that of her brother, was now over.

However Chrysostom made one last effort to please Uncle Lamyn, Margaret Mary's guardian, who wanted her to be a companion for his own daughter at Saint Ursula's. So he went to Mâcon to discuss her entrance and her dowry. Margaret's mother and other relatives all agreed with Chrysostom. But Margaret was dismayed, and sought refuge in prayer. As always, she turned to the Blessed Virgin Mary. As she tells us, she prayed to her "through the intermediary of St. Hyacinthe." She had Masses said in honor of our Blessed Lady. And finally, she received a clear answer from her: "Have no fear, you will be my true daughter and I shall always be your good Mother."

This answer might have been perfectly valid for her entrance at Saint Ursula's, but Margaret understood it as opposing it. For in her mind and in the language of the day, "The Saint Mary's" were the nuns of the Visitation.

When her brother returned from Mâcon, he told her: "They want a dowry of 4000 pounds. You can do whatever you want with your property, for the matter is not yet finally settled."

Margaret's answer came at once and in the most determined accents:

"It will never be settled. I want to go to the Saint Mary's, and enter a convent at some distance, where I shall have neither relative nor acquaintance, for I want to be a nun for love of God. I want to leave the world completely, by hiding in some little corner, to forget and be forgotten, and never to see it again."

There was no gainsaying her wishes. Several Visitation monasteries were mentioned to her. None of the names spoke to her heart. But then Paray-le-Monial was named! She was immediately conquered. She wanted Paray and nothing else. And yet, in order to get to Paray, she would have to pass through Charolles. How could she fail to visit the Urbanist Poor Clares who had educated her? Now, a new attack would be launched against her. When she admitted she was on her way to Paray-le-Monial, and going there to become a nun, the teachers at Charolles began to protest. She would never be able to endure the rigors of the rule! She would never be able to get used to it! At least, she should come back to Charolles when she realized her unfitness for the Visitation!

Margaret Mary defended herself as well as she could, and no argument could shake her resolve. As she wrote later on: "No matter what they told me, my heart remained unmoved, and became all the more resolute, continually saying: 'I must die or conquer.'"

So Margaret Mary completed her journey and finally arrived at Paray-le-Monial. This was where her Jesus wanted her.

In the next chapter we shall relate her impressions and first actions in this blessed monastery that now devoutly preserves her memory.

3

At the Visitation Monastery of Paray-le-Monial

"I SHALL NEVER BE ANYWHERE ELSE."

In the plans of divine wisdom, there must be certain predestined places: Bethlehem, Nazareth, Golgotha! Then, Rome, and all the places made sacred by the martyrs. And Hippo, and all the sees from which the Fathers of the Church taught. And of course, Avila, Paray-le-Monial, Ars, Lisieux, and so many others.

The minute Margaret Mary entered the Visitation of Paray she experienced a warmth around her heart. Let us quote her own words:

"From the instant I entered the parlor, I heard these words inwardly: 'This is where I want you!' After which I told my brother that we had to come to an understanding, since I would never be anywhere else!"

Her brother was taken by surprise at this decision. It had been agreed between them that he was only showing her one of the convents of the "Saint Mary's," but that there would be no question as yet of making a formal application for admittance. Margaret had promised everything asked of her. "But," she commented later, "I refused to go back home until everything was settled. After which, it seemed I had begun a new life, for I felt such great contentment and peace."

Again we see the same application of the "discernment of spirits." This peace and interior contentment seemed to her the sure sign of God's will. And yet nothing about her demeanor at that time gave external evidence of her religious vocation. Her friends and acquaintances, she tells us, made fun of her: "Look at her! Doesn't she act like a nun!" Indeed, she adds: "I wore more vain apparel than ever before, and ran after more pleasures because of the great joy I felt in seeing I now truly belonged totally to my sovereign Good!"

Until the end of her life, she could never thank Jesus enough for the many graces she had received from her earliest childhood, and above all for the grace of her religious vocation.

ENTERING THE CONVENT

After this first contact, she had to return home to set her affairs in order, dispose of her possessions, and make her final preparations. She overflowed with happiness. Everything she did was filled with holy impatience. And on June 20, 1671, Margaret left home forever to enter the convent. In another month, she would be twenty-four years old.

It was a Saturday, the day consecrated to the Blessed Virgin Mary. Two successive moods filled this memorable day. First, a wonderful inward joy resulting from her invincible resolve.

"Finally, the day I had so yearned for arrived when I said farewell to the world, and never have I felt so much joy or strength, that my heart was as though insensible to all the friendship as well as sorrow that everyone showed me, especially my mother. And I didn't shed a single tear as I left them, for I felt as if I were a slave who was being liberated from her prison and her chains, to enter the house of her Spouse, to possess Him and enjoy His presence in complete liberty, as well as His possessions and His love. This is what He said to my heart, which was completely beside itself, and I could give no reason for my vocation to the Saint Mary's, except that I wanted to be a daughter of the Blessed Virgin."

And yet could such joy be unmixed with anguish? St. Teresa of Avila relates that when she left her father's house after making a similar resolve, the dagger of her sacrifice transpierced her soul as she crossed the threshold of her home for the last time. In her words: "I experienced such anguish that I do not think I shall suffer any more at the hour of death. It seemed as though my bones were being pulled apart."

Margaret Mary in her turn experienced the same agony:

"But I admit that when the moment came to enter...all the sufferings I had had before and several others assailed me with such violence that it seemed as if my soul would separate from my body when I entered."

But within her, deep within her, the Master's voice made itself heard. He reminded her that He had broken the bonds of her captivity, that He wanted to clothe her with "the mantle of his joy" —the *vestimentum laetitiae* of which Scripture speaks in the Book of Judith (see Judith 16:8). So Margaret valiantly held back her overly human tears, and regained her truly supernatural joy. She could not help saying in a very loud voice, in fact, shouting: *"This is where God wants me!"*

It is quite clear that when she related these experiences many years later, her first impressions were confirmed by unforgettable revelations and, in spite of all the opposition we shall later describe, this monastery never ceased to lavish God's blessings upon her.

"At first I felt impressed upon my mind that this house of God was a holy place, that all those who lived in it had to be saints, that this name of Saint Mary indicated to me that it was necessary to be one whatever the cost and that this was why I had to abandon myself and sacrifice everything, without reservation or caution."

FIRST LESSONS

If anyone had asked her on that day how much she knew about the religious life, she would certainly have answered: "*Nothing at all!*" And indeed she knew nothing about it. Everything would be new for her. But as it happened, she already knew everything, for she had already been receiving for many years the most perfect preparation possible for her religious life. Everything she would now learn would echo resolutions she had already taken inwardly, desires she had already formulated, aspirations she had already long held.

Margaret Mary knew she wanted to be a saint, *had to be a saint.* As she later said: "This made everything that first seemed hardest for me easier."

At first she probably didn't even understand the Latin formulas in common usage at the convent. But she did her best to obey them, and that was enough for her:

"For a few days, every morning I was awakened with these words that I heard distinctly without understanding them: *Dilexisti justitiam*[1] and the rest of the verse. At other times: *Audi, filia, et vide,* etc., and also these words: 'You have recognized your path and your way, O my Jerusalem, house of Israel! But the Lord will keep you in all your ways and will never abandon you!'

"I used to tell all this to my good mistress, without understanding it. I used to think of her, and my

1. These words are taken from Psalm 45, verse 8 (Psalm 44 in the Vulgate), part of the "royal epithalamium," that is, the nuptial hymn of the Bridegroom and his Bride: "You love justice and hate wickedness; therefore God, your God, has anointed you with the oil of gladness...."

The words *Audi filia et vide* were from the same Psalm (45:11) and mean: "Hear, O daughter, and see; turn your ear, forget your people and your father's house."

superior too, as my Jesus Christ upon earth. And as I...had never had any guidance or direction, I was so happy to see myself subjected to it, in order to obey, that everything they said to me seemed so many oracles. And so I felt there was nothing more to fear so long as I did everything under obedience."

It is quite true, therefore, that she knew nothing, and yet knew everything. For she knew she had only to follow, to obey, and then everything would lead her to the divine Master.

As we have noted, she saw her "good mistress" as the representative of Jesus Christ. She was referring, of course, to her mistress of novices. It was under her direction that she began her life as a nun, and so we must learn more about her as well as about the entire community at Paray-le-Monial.

THE NOVITIATE AND THE COMMUNITY

When Margaret Mary entered the Monastery of the Visitation, there were thirty-three choir sisters, plus five lay sisters, three sisters at the turn, and three novices.

The mistress of novices was Sister Ann Frances Thouvant, a former superior—or as was customary to say in the Order, "the very honored deposed Sister." She was also the nun who had been longest in the convent. Professed there forty-four years before, she had been superior four times. She had known St. Jane Frances de Chantal, the revered foundress. According to some of the Order's chronicles: "She had attracted the foundress' attention... in her various sojourns at Paray." The same chronicles add: "The virtues she practiced during her long religious career were one more proof of the clear judgment of our holy Mother in the discernment of spirits."

In the summer of 1671, Sister Ann Frances performed the cumulative functions of assistant superior, counselor, and mistress of novices, at one and the same time. It was her responsibility to guide Margaret Mary's first steps in the religious life, and she did so with a vigor and authority born of extensive experience and strong character.

The monastery was governed by Mother Margaret Jeromia Hersant, who belonged to the Monastery of St. Anthony in Paris. She would soon complete her term as superior at Paray, go from there to Châlons as superior, and then return to her Paris convent in 1678, where she was to die in 1679.

In the novitiate, Margaret Mary's companions were Sister Ann Jeromina Piedenuz, Sister Ann Liduvinia Rosselin, who was a very fervent and sensitive soul, and Sister Frances Catherine Carme du Chailloux. The first and third of these nuns died young. The second lived until 1702.

In the community as a whole, it would be easy to name nuns of exceptional holiness. By and large, this was a very fervent monastery. Although Margaret Mary was to experience much opposition from certain of her sisters, we can be sure this did not stem from jealousy, or ill will, but from a very legitimate distrust of what were called "extraordinary ways," as well as a somewhat narrow and exclusive attachment to the customs of the Order and a quite natural dislike of innovations.

Above all, in all of this opposition which caused Margaret Mary so much suffering because of her very sensitive nature, we must see a special disposition of Christ who wanted His deeply-loved spouse to share His cross.

At any rate, we know that the young aspirant who had asked admission to Paray had only one desire: to obey. We have said she thought she knew nothing and had everything to learn. What, therefore, was her first request? She has told us in her own words.

MENTAL PRAYER

Margaret Mary said, referring to her mistress of novices:

"When I begged her to teach me mental prayer, for which my soul felt such great hunger, she refused to believe that anyone who entered religion—that is, the convent—at the age of twenty-three, didn't know how to practice it. And after I had assured her I didn't, she said to me the first time: *'Go and place yourself before our Lord like a canvas waiting before a painter.'*"

This was a magnificent formula. But it seemed obscure to the poor young aspirant. So she went away pensively and prayed to her Jesus to come and help her.

"I would have wanted her to explain what she was saying to me, as I didn't understand it, and I didn't dare tell her. But these words were said to me: *'Come, I shall teach you.'*"

She placed herself in thought before her Savior. And then everything became clear to her:

"And as soon as I was engaged in mental prayer, my sovereign Master made me see that my soul was this *canvas waiting*, on which He wanted to paint all the marks of His suffering life, which was spent in love and privation, in separation, silence and sacrifice, until its consummation; that He would impress this image upon my soul, after having purified it of all its remaining blemishes, including affection for earthly things and self-love, to which I was very much inclined by natural temperament."

THE NIGHT

If Margaret Mary had known St. John of the Cross, she would have understood that her divine Master wanted above all to initiate her into the night of the senses and the night of the spirit, that is to say, into a total renouncement of nature so as to belong to Him alone.

But precisely because Margaret Mary most certainly did not know the writings of the great theologian of the mystical life, we are all the more amazed at the remarkable similarity between the two "nights" of John of the Cross and the states into which Jesus introduced her:

"He stripped me of everything in that moment, and after emptying my heart and baring my soul, He kindled in me such a great desire to love Him and to suffer that He pursued me and gave me no rest, and I could think only of finding ways to love Him by crucifying myself...."

And yet with admirable wisdom she told her mistress of novices about her excessive zeal. On one occasion, she had planned to interpret her mistress' permission to practice certain penances far more broadly than was intended. In short, she was tempted to use deception toward her mistress for the purpose of nailing herself more securely to the cross of Jesus.

Margaret Mary was certainly sincere in her intentions, but she was on very dangerous ground. "Self-will" was about to win the day within her over the spirit of discipline and obedience. She has assured us that she was preserved from this peril by St. Francis de Sales in person:

"Having determined to do this, my holy Founder reprimanded me severely, and would not let me continue, so that I have never had the courage to return to it, for his words have always remained engraved in my heart: 'Indeed, my daughter, do you think you can please God by exceeding the limits of obedience, which is the principal support and foundation of this Congregation, and not austerities?'"

We cannot lay too much stress on these words and on the entire episode. Her whole life was to be dominated by the spirit of obedience. She would never want to do anything except under command.

And as we shall see, Jesus Himself was to command her to obey her superiors rather than His own private revelations. Indeed, there is nothing more important in the spiritual life than this perfect submission of what might be called private inspirations to the supreme wisdom of the Church, represented by legitimate superiors.

THE HABIT, THE FIRST TRIALS

After just over two months, on August 25, 1671, Margaret Mary, until then only an aspirant, received the holy habit of the Visitation. Among those present were her mother, her brother Chrysostom, her uncle, and the pastor of Vérosvres. They signed the attestation declaring it was "of her own free will and without any constraint whatsoever" that she was committing herself to the religious life. As she saw it, receiving the habit was the celebration of her divine engagement. She then began her novitiate that was supposed to last an entire year. Before she could be allowed to pronounce her vows, she would need the consent of her superiors and of her sisters in religion.

For Margaret Mary, trials were not long in coming. God was lavishing His graces upon her. But this very fact made her behave in a manner that baffled the community. She told everything to her mistress of novices, and the latter had doubts about what was happening to her new novice. She kept trying to make her understand that "this was not the spirit of the daughters of Saint Mary, who wanted nothing extraordinary" from them. She even added that if Margaret Mary *"didn't give all that up, she would not be accepted!"*

Now the young novice was in deep desolation. Try as she might to conform to the customs of the Order, it was wasted effort. She found it impossible to follow the methods of mental prayer in use at the convent. She would always come back to the method her mistress of novices had suggested to her from the first, namely, remaining before her Jesus like a "*canvas waiting.*" Sister Thouvant had not really meant it quite as Margaret Mary interpreted it. She could not believe that a beginner had already advanced beyond the obligatory phase of the *active way.* She spared no effort to make her pass through this phase, which is common to beginners. Every means was used to rescue the poor child from her inexplicable attraction toward sublime modes of prayer that could well be delusory.

Let us not rashly judge this as a deliberate persecution. The nuns of the Visitation had only the best of intentions. They were surprised, they were seeking to understand, they were studying her case. Their criterion of comparison was their own experience as a community and its established rules. In order to provide her with material occupations that could draw her away from what they feared might be ecstasies of suspicious origin, she was placed under the guidance of an "officer" who made her work during times of mental prayer. Then, when she asked her mistress to allow her to engage in mental prayer, the latter would reprimand her severely and tell her to pray as she worked at the various tasks of the novitiate.

Margaret Mary obeyed, and later related that "nothing could distract her from her sweet joy and consolation of soul, which continued to grow." And so more radical means were used, always with the purpose of bringing her "down to earth," so to speak.

"I was commanded to go and listen to the points of mental prayer for the morning, after which I would go out to sweep whatever room I was told."

This might continue until Prime, that is, throughout the hour devoted by the community as a whole to the exercise of mental prayer in the chapel. Afterward, she had to go and give an account of her mental prayer to the mistress of novices. But once again the level of her mental prayer was so lofty that the nuns couldn't understand what was going on.

Finally there was no denying the evidence. Margaret Mary never did anything without obeying! It was also known, by her own admission, that she wanted nothing so much as to suffer for her Jesus. As she later said: "I felt an insatiable hunger for humiliations and mortifications." And she asked her divine Master to see that she got some. But even this request, which was always refused, gave her a noble reason for shame: the shame of begging and the shame of being refused.

However, one day the Lord permitted her to be put to the most rigorous test. Outwardly, it seemed a trivial matter, just about the most trivial imaginable.

Margaret Mary didn't like cheese. In fact, she has said that her entire family had an invincible aversion for this valuable and common food. Her brother Chrysostom had gone so far as to include in her contract of admission to the Visitation that she would not be made to eat cheese. In itself, this was such a small matter that no objection had been raised to this provision. But a day came when the nun in charge of the refectory inadvertently gave Margaret Mary—just as everyone else—a piece of cheese. The young novice saw in this an indication of God's will and considered it her duty to obey. But nature was stronger than her will, and she could not overcome her strong revulsion. The mistress of novices took careful note.

After the meal, she took Margaret Mary aside and chided her for her cowardice. Margaret Mary for her part shamefacedly promised to be more valiant the next time. For three days she continued to fight her aversion, and each day her courage failed. As she later said: "I was dying of shame not to be able to overcome my nature." In a despairing tone, she said to her mistress of novices: "Alas! If only you could take my life rather than let me fail in obedience!"

But the good mistress was determined to carry through the experiment to the end. So she said in a dry voice: "Come, now! You were not worthy of practicing it, and I now forbid what I commanded you to do earlier!" Later on, our saint told the sequel to this incident, as follows:

"That was enough for me. First I said: 'I must die or conquer!' I went before the most Blessed Sacrament, my ordinary refuge, where I remained about three or four hours weeping and sighing, to obtain the strength to overcome: 'Alas! my God, have You abandoned me? Indeed, is there still some reservation in my sacrifice and is it not completely consummated as a perfect holocaust?' But my Lord, wanting to test my heart's fidelity to Him to the end, as He later made me see, took pleasure in seeing His unworthy slave combat divine love against natural revulsions. In the end He was victorious, for with no other consolation or arms than these words: 'Love must have no reservations!', I went and fell on my knees before my mistress, asking her to permit me through mercy to do what she had first wanted of me. And finally, I did it, although I have never felt such revulsion, which always recurred whenever I had to do it, and this has continued for about eight years."

The testimony we have on this subject from various individuals states that "she was a pitiful sight." After eating cheese, she was practically overcome with illness until evening. It was not until eight years later that she stopped eating cheese, and then only at the strict injunction of her superiors.

Anyone who shares Margaret Mary's aversion to cheese will agree that perhaps Francis of Assisi gained no greater merit when he kissed the leper's sores.

HER PROFESSION DEFERRED

After making this sacrifice—and we can assume there were others as well—Margaret Mary received so many graces of prayer and love that she felt obliged to say to her Jesus: "O my God, hold back this torrent that is engulfing me, or increase my capacity to receive it!"

But when she faithfully related this to her mistress of novices, it occasioned new fears. She was told it was quite obvious she had no aptitude for the spirit of the Visitation. In fact, her spiritual ways might be nothing but delusions.

What sorrow for the young novice! So they were going to send her away! "Alas, my Lord!" she sighed, "will You be the cause of my being sent away?"

Jesus' answer was not long in coming. As always, He made her submit to the path of obedience: "Tell your superior that she has nothing to fear in accepting you, that I am answerable for you, and that if she thinks I am solvent I shall be your guarantee."

It was a difficult message for Margaret Mary to deliver. However, she did it with her usual docility. Somewhat disconcerted, the mistress of novices commanded her to ask the Lord, "as a sign of His pledge," to make her useful to holy religion—that is to say, to the religious life of the convent—"by the exact practice of all its observances." Jesus answered:

"Well, my daughter, I grant you all that, for I shall make you more useful to religion[1] than she thinks, but in a way that is as yet known only to me. And from now on I shall adapt my graces to the spirit of your rule, to the will of your superiors and to your weakness, so that you may consider suspect everything that turns you away from the exact prac-

1. We think this word should be taken here as a synonym of religious life in the convent. Margaret Mary was to be more useful to the Visitation than anyone could yet surmise, but in a way still unknown to everyone, including herself.

tice of the rule, which I want you to prefer to everything else. In addition, I am pleased that you should prefer the will of your superiors to mine, when they forbid you to do what I have commanded.

"Let them do everything they want with you: I shall certainly be able to find a way to make my plans succeed, even by means that seem so opposed and contrary to them. And I reserve for myself only the direction of your interior life and especially of your heart, in which, after I have established the reign of my pure love, I shall never yield to others!"

Margaret Mary's superiors realized they were dealing with an exceptional and unique situation. Now, her words completely reassured them. Obedience was safeguarded all along the line. From that time on, the new superior, Mother Mary Frances de Saumaise, and the mistress of novices, Sister Thouvant, realized that this young novice was a privileged soul. The sincere humility that shone through her words and actions could not deceive.

To be doubly sure, Mother de Saumaise consulted her former superior at Dijon, Mother Boulier. When the latter was told what was going on at Paray, she recognized in the young nun certain states that she herself had experienced. Her advice was categorical. Without hesitation she answered that Margaret's ways were truly from God, that this was an authentic vocation, and that the Visitation at Paray should accept her. Mother de Saumaise was delighted with this decision, and she related it to Sister Thouvant, still hesitant but already partially convinced.

While these consultations went on, Margaret Mary's novitiate year came to an end on August 25, 1672. It was with great dismay that she saw this date pass without being called to take the veil. So there had been a negative vote in the community against her admission! However, Mother de Saumaise' authority, supported by Mother Boulier's judgment and that of the mistress of novices, brought about a complete change of view in the community, or at least among the sisters who made up the governing council. And so, after a delay of two months and a few days, Margaret was finally allowed to pronounce her vows. This occurred on November 6, 1672.

THE LAST TRIAL

Before the great day arrived, Margaret Mary had to undergo another trial. Here again, as always, she revealed her great spirit of obedience. On October 27th, she had begun what was called her "solitude," that is, a ten-day retreat in preparation for her vows. On All Souls' Day, November 2nd, she knelt before the Blessed Sacrament "to make reparation for the abuses she had committed against His graces," and offered herself as a holocaust to her divine Master. He replied:

"Remember that it is a crucified God you intend to wed. That is why you must conform to Him, by bidding farewell to all the pleasures of life, for there will be no more pleasures for you except those transpierced with the cross."

Our Lord was announcing to Margaret Mary that He had chosen her to share in His own sacrifice as a victim of reparation.

It so happened that her superiors decided to subject her, the great contemplative, to a severe trial of humility. In the convent enclosure, they kept a she-ass and her foal. They could have tied them up, to keep them from tearing up the vegetable garden. Instead, they decided to have the novices watch these two animals. We should note that Margaret Mary was not singled out by a humiliating choice in this instance. This task was to be shared by all the novices. But she took it more to heart than any of the others. Except for the periods when she was in choir, she considered it her duty to remain constantly in the enclosure. But let us read what she has to say about her inner emotions on this occasion:

"I gave no thought to time or place since my Sovereign accompanied me everywhere. It mattered not at all to me what I might be assigned to do.... I experienced this when I was told to make my retreat for my profession watching a she-ass with her little foal in the garden, which gave me quite a bit of exercise, for I was not allowed to tie her up and they wanted me to keep her in a small corner that had been marked out, lest she do some damage, and the two animals did nothing but run. I had no rest until the evening Angelus when I came in for supper. And then during part of Matins, I would return to the stable to feed her."

For a contemplative, these were very mundane and absorbing duties. But our saint was perfectly content to carry them out.

"I was so happy in this occupation that I would not have cared if it had continued for the rest of my life. And my Sovereign kept me company so faithfully that all the running I had to do didn't hamper me at all, for it was there I received such great graces, that I had never experienced any like them before."

What were these graces? She was to tell us they were beyond human expression, but we can glimpse them from her words: "Above all, what He made me understand concerning the mystery of His holy passion and death."

And she concludes:

"But it is an abyss to write about.... I shall only say that this is what has given me so great a love for the cross, that I cannot live a single instant without suffering, but suffering in silence, without consolation, relief or compassion, and dying with this Sovereign of my soul, crushed under the cross by every sort of shame, humiliation, rejection and scorn."

CONFESSION AND RESOLUTIONS

The *Directory* used by the mistress of novices states that she would be well advised to recommend that her daughters make a general confession of their past life before pronouncing their vows, so as to better prepare themselves to enter a totally new life. Sister Thouvant conformed to this usage, and Margaret Mary eagerly seized this opportunity to purify even more a conscience already very pure.

As we remember, she had made a similar confession at Vérosvres, at which time she was so filled with scruples that she had copied all the sins listed in the examination of conscience suggested in a book, for fear of forgetting any at all. Now she was again filled with anxiety. But she was far more advanced in the spiritual life. Besides, she had trained herself so well never to do anything without consulting the divine Presence dwelling in her heart, that she received the following reassuring answer from Jesus:

"Why do you fret so? Do what you can. I shall supplement what is lacking, for what I desire most in this sacrament is a contrite and humbled heart which admits its guilt without subterfuge, out of a sincere resolve to displease me no more."

She had obviously made great progress in her fight against scruples. The voice that spoke so often deep in her heart, the voice of her Jesus, was the voice of wisdom and inner peace.

She therefore obeyed this advice. When the priest raised his hand over her to give her absolution, she later recalled: "I seemed to see and feel myself stripped, then clothed in a white dress, with these words: 'Here is the robe of innocence in which I clothe your soul, so that you may live only by the life of a God-man, that is, so that you may live as though no longer living, but letting me live in you.'"

In addition, we have the retreat resolutions she made on this eve of her profession, and which were to be the rule of her interior life from that time on.

A study of these resolutions will be of the greatest value in understanding her spirituality:

"Here are my resolutions which must last all my life, since my Beloved has dictated them Himself. After I received Him in my heart, He said to me:

" 'Here is the wound in my side, so that you may make of it your present and perpetual dwelling. There you will be able to preserve the robe of innocence in which I have clothed your soul, that you may live henceforth by the life of a God-man, as though no longer living, so that I may live perfectly in you.' "

These first lines of her resolutions clearly outline the goal to be attained. It is impossible to aim any higher. This was the goal referred to by St. John of the Cross in the following verse from one of his *Spiritual Canticles:*

"The beloved transformed into her Beloved!"

And while Margaret Mary probably never had any direct knowledge of the writings of this great master of the mystical life, she was proceeding by exactly the same rules under the guidance of her Jesus. As we have already said, these rules were the night of the senses and the night of the soul.

Here is what her resolutions had to say about the night of the senses:

"Think about your body and about everything that will happen to you as if they no longer existed; act as though no longer acting, but I alone in you. To this end, your powers and your senses must remain buried in me; you must be deaf, mute, blind, and insensible to all earthly things...."

And here is what her resolutions say about the night of the soul:

"Will as though no longer willing, without judging, or desiring, with no affection or will except the will of my good pleasure, in which must consist your every delight; seek nothing outside of me, if you do not want to insult my power and offend me grievously, since I want to be all things to you."

The resolutions conclude as follows:

"Be always disposed to receive me; I shall always be ready to give myself to you, because you will often be delivered up to the fury of your enemies. But have no fear, I will surround you with my power and be the prize of your victories. Take care never to open your eyes to look at yourself outside of *me. Let your motto be to love and suffer blindly: one heart, one love, one God!"*

After these lines, the young nun wrote out the following promises, in her own blood:

"I, pitiful and miserable nothingness, protest to my God that I submit and sacrifice myself to everything He asks of me, immolating my heart for the fulfillment of His good pleasure, without reserving any interest other than His greater glory and His pure love, to which I consecrate and abandon my entire being and my every moment.

"I belong forever to my beloved; I am forever His slave, His servant and His creature, since He is all mine, and I am His unworthy spouse, Sister Margaret Mary, dead to the world. Everything from God and nothing from me; everything God's and nothing mine; everything for God and nothing for me!"

It is impossible not to discover in these words the famous *Todo y Nada* (Everything and Nothing) of St. John of the Cross.

With dispositions such as these, the young nun was certainly well prepared to make her vows, as indeed she did on November 6, 1672.

4

The Great Revelations

THE DIVINE PRESENCE

What was the immediate effect of Margaret Mary's total gift to her Lord and God? She has related it very briefly in the following lines of her *Autobiography:*

"Having finally attained the benefit of holy profession I had so much desired, it was on that day that my divine Master deigned to accept me as His spouse, but in a way I feel powerless to express. All I can say is that He spoke to me and treated me *like a spouse of Tabor,* and this was harder for me to bear than death, as I saw I did not conform to my Spouse, whom I pictured totally disfigured and lacerated on Calvary."

These two aspects were to characterize her interior life from that time on. On the one hand, she received extraordinary interior illuminations, supernatural disclosures, such as a husband makes to a greatly loved spouse. And on the other hand, she was intensely aware of her own smallness, her nothingness, her unworthiness, in the presence of such a Spouse.

She was to retain two sentiments all her life: boundless trust, and ever-growing humility. When we read her beautiful letters, it is impossible not to be moved and sometimes troubled by her continual use of expressions she felt were indispensable to humble and shame herself, such as references to her unworthiness, or saying she was a paltry creature, a hypocrite of whom everyone should beware.

We cannot help wondering how she could feel so miserable when she was favored with so many supernatural favors. Here again it will help us to turn to St. John of the Cross. "When a ray of sunshine goes through a very clean window, it reveals atoms of dust everywhere in the air. When the love of God enters a soul, this soul sees countless imperfections in itself."

Now, the most immediate result of Margaret Mary's profession was a sense of Jesus' "*presence,*" which was a most wonderful new experience for her. And that is certainly what she means when she assures us that her divine Master spoke to her and treated her "like a wife of Tabor."

"From that time on, He favored me with His divine presence, but in a way that I had never yet experienced; for I had never received such a great grace, as far as the effects it has always worked in me since then...."[1]

How far did this blessed sense of "presence" go? She has told it in the most forceful language:

"I would see Him, feel Him so close to me, and hear Him much better than through my bodily senses, which would have allowed me to turn my attention away from Him. But I could offer no impediment to this [presence], since I had no [active] participation in it at all."

This divine presence was so intense that she would humble herself more and more whenever she spoke to her Jesus:

"But this was said to me: 'Let me do each thing in its own time, for now I want you to be the toy

1. She wrote this in 1686 or 1687, three or four years before her death, and fourteen or fifteen years after her profession.

of my love, wishing to play with you according to my good pleasure, like children with their dolls. You must be abandoned, without plans or resistance, allowing me to find pleasure at your expense, but you will not be the loser.'

"He promised never to leave me, saying: 'Always be ready and eager to receive me, for I want to make my dwelling in you, to converse and talk with you.'"

Many saints have had such experiences, and they have all agreed that the immediate fruit of this adorable presence is a sentiment of extraordinary smallness before it. This was what Moses had experienced in the desert in the presence of the burning bush.

A voice called out: "Moses! Moses!" And he answered: "Here I am." The voice continued: "Come no nearer! Remove the sandals from your feet, for the place where you stand is holy ground. I am the God of your father, the God of Abraham, the God of Isaac, the God of Jacob." And Moses "hid his face, for he was afraid to look at God" (Ex. 3:4-6).

The presence of God is at once delightful and overwhelming. Let us listen to what Margaret Mary has to say about it:

"It impressed such a deep sense of abasement within me that I felt as though I had been swallowed up in the abyss of my nothingness, from which I have never been able to come forth, out of respect and homage for this infinite greatness in whose presence I would want to remain always on my knees or with my face pressed to the ground. And this is what I have done, as far as my various duties and my weakness have permitted, for He has allowed me no rest in a less respectful posture, and I have not dared sit down except when someone else was present, because He has given me such an awareness of my unworthiness that I have felt embarrassed to be seen, and wished no one would even remember me any more, except to scorn me, humiliate me, and say insulting things to me, since I have no right to anything but that."

Thus, she was forearmed against the opposition and contradictions she would encounter in carrying out a mission that was still unknown to her. She was to find a way of remaining unswervingly faithful to her Master's commands and of doing everything He asked. At the same time, she had no trouble accepting opposition, criticism, objections, and even persecutions, because she thought they were really due to her sins, and that she was the only obstacle to the Lord's mercy.

"This one love of my soul was so delighted to see me treated in this way that, in spite of the sensitivity of my proud nature, He allowed me no pleasure among creatures except on these occasions of contradiction, humiliation, and abjection, which were delightful food to me, and He never left me in want of such food or said 'That's enough!' On the contrary, He Himself did whatever others or I myself failed to do."

TWO KINDS OF HOLINESS

Taught by God Himself, the young nun embarked quite easily upon the path of holiness, "the royal road of the holy cross," to use the words of the author of *The Imitation of Christ.*

The Church has canonized Margaret Mary and accepted her message concerning public devotion to the Sacred Heart because it has recognized in her the authentic tradition of the highest Christian mysticism. This is the tradition contained in our Gospels, especially the Gospel of St. John, and the Letters of St. Paul and the other apostles. Once again, let us turn to her *Autobiography.* From beginning to end, it echoes the Gospel theme of love for souls.

"He honored me with His conversations, like a friend or a husband who was most passionately in love, or like a father wounded with love for his only child, and in other ways too. I shall not speak of the effects this produced in me. All I will say is that He made me see in Him two kinds of holiness, a holiness of love and another of justice, each very rigorous in its own way, and continually exercised over me. The first made me suffer a kind of purgatory very painful to endure, to relieve the holy souls who were detained there, and whom He would permit, according to His good pleasure, to speak to me. And His holiness of justice, so terrible and terrifying for sinners, made me feel its just rigor, making me suffer for sinners, and, He said, 'especially for the souls who are consecrated to me, for whose sake I shall make you see and feel later on what it will be good for you to suffer for love of me.'"

AN ORDINARY AND YET EXTRAORDINARY WAY

Obviously, Margaret Mary's vocation was an exceptional one, and this very fact was to bring her great humiliation within her community. Indeed, it would be totally false to imagine that the religious in convents are eagerly seeking the most extraordinary supernatural experiences. The exact opposite is true. And it is in the spirit of the Church to distrust everything that lies outside the ordinary ways of sanctification. No one was more severe than St. John of the Cross in passing judgment on visions, revelations, prophecies, and other "spectacular" matters.

But Margaret Mary's humble obedience to her superiors was a corrective that eliminated any danger of illuminism on her part. The same had been true a century earlier of St. Teresa of Avila. Margaret Mary hid nothing from her superiors, as she has declared. Very often she did not even understand everything she was telling them in the name of her Jesus. They, for their part, didn't know what to think of this young nun thus led by God, and feared she was suffering from delusions. She feared this more than anyone else:

"As they had explained to me that these were extraordinary ways unsuited to Daughters of Saint Mary, I was greatly grieved and used every kind of resistance in my power to give up this way."

So we see there was no complacency, no pride, on Margaret Mary's part, but only a great fear of being the plaything of the devil who might be presenting himself to her as an angel of light. Further, we know she made every effort to conform to the advice given her. It was all wasted energy. She was no longer in command of her powers. She was now experiencing the blessed bending of the faculties that is the mark of lofty contemplation.

"I made every effort to diligently follow the method of mental prayer that was being taught me along with the other practices, but nothing would stick in my mind. Although I read my points of mental prayer, everything would vanish and I could learn and retain only what my divine Master taught me, and this caused me great suffering."

Here was great suffering indeed, the suffering of being different, of not being able to follow the same path as everybody else, and of incurring, as a result, the reproach of the superiors whom she venerated and loved.

Margaret Mary was putting up a valiant fight. Jesus watched her, no doubt with a smile. Her magnificent obedience conformed so well to His wishes. And yet He took care not to deliver her from such rare and precious trials.

"And I used to complain to Him: 'O my sovereign Master! Why don't You leave me in the ordinary vocation of the Daughters of Saint Mary? Have You brought me into Your holy house to destroy me? Give these extraordinary graces to chosen souls who will cooperate more fully with them and give You greater glory than I, who do nothing but resist You.

I want only Your love and Your cross, and that is all I need to be a good nun. That is all I desire.'

"And the answer I received was this:

"'Keep fighting, my daughter. I am satisfied with you. And we shall see who wins the victory, the Creator or His creature, strength or weakness, the Almighty or the powerless. But he who conquers will be the victor forever.'"

This answer from Jesus left Margaret Mary greatly troubled. But she persisted in her resolve to want only obedience, to fight against everything that seemed to endanger obedience. And in this, too, she was following the Gospel. Jesus frankly told her so:

"Learn that I am not offended by all your fighting and opposition to me for the sake of obedience. Was it not for obedience that I gave my life? But I want to teach you that I am the absolute Master of my gifts and of my creatures, and that nothing can keep me from carrying out my plans. That is why not only do I want you to do whatever your superiors will tell you, but also that you should do nothing at all that I shall command you without their consent. For I love obedience, and without it no one can be pleasing to me."

THE WAY OF FREEDOM

After colloquies such as these, Margaret Mary used to go and tell everything to her superior, good Mother de Saumaise. We can surmise the great anxiety the holy nun must have experienced. For it was certainly her duty to be on the lookout for any possible flights of imagination by such a young sister. But it was also her duty not to be an impediment to God's will for one of His creatures. In such a situation, how was she to practice "the discernment of spirits"? What could be more reassuring than Sister Margaret Mary's perfect obedience, her constant humility and sincerity, her resolve to obey at all costs?

Following the dictates of sound judgment, the superior decided in favor of Margaret Mary:

"This pleased my superior, and she told me to abandon myself to the power, and this I did with great joy and peace...."

So the preparation continued for Margaret Mary's mission. Indeed, all that was then happening within her can only be interpreted as a supernatural preparation for the mission she would soon be called upon to carry out.

In this preparation we always find the same elements: continual and holy demands on Christ's part, great distrust of herself, as well as humility and a desire for immolation. As yet she knew nothing whatever about any private devotion to the Sacred Heart, and even less about any message to be transmitted to the entire Church on this subject. But everything was leading her toward that mysterious point which would be the secret of her whole life.

INTERIOR DIALOGUE

She has given us a striking example of the type of interior dialogues she engaged in with her Jesus:

"After Holy Communion He asked me to repeat for Him the sacrifice I had already made to Him of my freedom and my whole being, and this I did with all my heart.

"'Provided, my sovereign Master, You let nothing extraordinary appear outwardly about me, except what can cause me humiliation and abjection before creatures, and destroy me in their esteem, for, alas! my God, I realize my weakness, I fear to betray You, and that Your gifts may not be in safekeeping within me!'

"'Have no fear, my daughter,' He said to me, 'I shall keep them in good order, for I myself shall be their guardian and shall make you powerless to resist me.'

"'Indeed, my God! Will You leave me always free of suffering?'

"First, I was shown a large cross, whose end I could not see, but it was all covered with flowers:

"'This is the bed of my chaste spouses, where I shall make you consummate the delights of my heart: little by little these flowers will fall and you will have only thorns, which are now hidden because of your weakness. But they will prick you so hard that you will need all the strength of my love to endure the pain of it.'"

For a soul less generous than Margaret Mary, such an announcement might have been a cause for terror. But God had been preparing her so well since childhood that now she could want only the cross, so as to more closely resemble her Jesus. This is how she herself has expressed it:

"These words made me very happy, because I thought there would never be enough sufferings, humiliations, or scorn to quench my burning thirst for them,[1] and because *I would never be able to find a greater suffering than what I experienced in not suffering enough.* For His love left me no rest day or night, but His sufferings grieved me. *I wanted the cross pure and unadulterated,* and to this end I would have wanted to see my body continually crushed by austerities or labors, of which I took as much as my strength would bear, for I could not live for a moment without suffering. The more I suffered, the more I satisfied this holiness of love that had kindled three desires in my heart which tormented me incessantly: one was the desire to suffer, the second was the desire to love Him and to receive Communion, and the third was to die so as to be united to Him."

She said: "*I wanted the cross pure and unadulterated.*" But we must realize that her will was per-

1. It goes without saying that this very thirst was a grace, in fact, one of the greatest of all. St. Augustine has said very eloquently that God "perfects His gifts within us."

fectly obedient in all things to her divine Spouse. We should note here that in her letters and reflections she often uses the motto given to her Order by its founder, the wise St. Francis de Sales: "Ask nothing and refuse nothing." This wisdom was confirmed to Margaret Mary by Jesus in person, for she needed to temper her excessive zeal during the early years of her religious life.

As this is a lesson of major importance, we shall discuss it at some length.

MODERATION

Margaret Mary certainly knew that Jesus abhors the cowardly and the tepid. But her temptation was not in this direction. Her tendency, which we have already noticed during her childhood, was toward exaggeration and excess.

Jesus continually reproved her on this point. She has recorded the lessons He taught her in very clear terms. This is what He said to her:

"You are mistaken in thinking you can please me by these kinds of actions and mortifications, chosen through self-will, which forces the superior's will to yield rather than give them up. Oh! understand that I reject all that as fruit corrupted by self-will, which I hold in horror in the soul of a religious. And I would prefer her to enjoy all her little comforts under obedience, than to crush herself with austerities and fasts chosen by her self-will."

This amounted to saying that mortifications of the spirit are more meritorious before God than those of the body.

Margaret Mary had a proof of it in various circumstances when she thought she was doing the right thing without regard for obedience.

She relates this incident: "Once when I had finished an *Ave maris stella* as a discipline, He said to me: 'This is my part.' And as I was continuing:

'That's the devil's part you are doing now.' And so I stopped at once.

"And another time, for the souls in purgatory, the moment I wanted to do more than I had permission to do, they surrounded me and complained that I was hitting them. This made me resolve to die rather than exceed the limits of obedience in even the smallest degree, for, after that, He would make me do penance for it."

The moral is clear. No excesses of zeal! This is the rule her Master imposed on her. And He also made her understand that He demands absolute fidelity to even the smallest regulations of the religious life.

"What He reprimanded most severely was lack of respect and attention before the most Blessed Sacrament, especially during the time of the Office and mental prayer, lack of honesty and purity in one's intentions, vain curiosity."

AT THE INFIRMARY

It is customary in a convent to divide responsibilities and functions among the nuns. The day after her profession, Margaret Mary was given an "obedience." She was assigned as nurse's aide to Sister Catherine August Marest, an excellent religious, but with an active, officious, and fiery temperament.

Margaret Mary, on the contrary, was calm, composed, a little slow in her movements. She was also rather awkward, which was a more serious matter. The American philosopher William James has referred to her in his famous book, *Religious Experience*. Being a matter-of-fact and practical man, he expressed ironic commiseration for this "saint" who too often let the dishes fall out of her hands and broke everything she touched. Those around her and she herself were quick to say that the devil had something to do with it.

"He would often make me fall and break everything I had in my hands, and then he would make fun of me, sometimes even laughing in my face: 'Oh! the clumsy one! You'll never do anything worthwhile!' And that would cast my spirits down into such great melancholy and depression that I didn't know what to do! For he often took away my ability to tell our mother about it, because obedience crushed and dispelled all his power."

It seems the devil went even further, for he tried unsuccessfully to kill her:

"Once he pushed me from the top of a staircase when I was holding a full earthenware jar, but I didn't spill any of it, and I found myself at the bottom of the staircase unharmed, although those who saw me fall thought I had broken my legs; but I felt my faithful guardian holding me up."

Later, when she wrote about her assignment in the infirmary, she said: "God alone can know how much I had to suffer there!"

But it was partly her own fault! Hadn't she begged our Lord not to let anything appear outwardly in her demeanor except "what could cause her the most humiliation and abjection before creatures, and destroy her in their esteem"?

Certainly, justice was done to her in later years. When we read her letters or her advice to the novices whom she was in charge of training for a considerable period of time, we find she expressed herself in a clear, precise, firm spirit, using a simple, uniform but pleasant style, and practical wisdom. It does not therefore surprise us to read in her first biography, written by Father Croiset soon after her death:

"God had given her wit and intellect, sound and penetrating judgment."

One of her superiors, Mother Greyfié, who succeeded Mother de Saumaise, declared that she was "a subject very well qualified to succeed in everything, if the Lord had not granted her request to be unknown and hidden in abjection and suffering."

So, in spite of William James, let us not take these stories about broken dishes too seriously. Rather, let us turn to the "amazing graces" that were granted to this servant of the Lord.

THE FIRST GREAT REVELATION

Margaret Mary had often been privileged to hear interior "locutions" in which Jesus invited her to contemplate the open wound in His side. In view of her devotion to her crucified Savior, her mind turned with tender sorrow to all the sacred wounds of Christ, and by preference to the wound opened in His side by the soldier's lance.

Many saints, both men and women, had meditated on this before her. Devotion to the Sacred Heart had always existed in some form in the Church. But it was reserved for Margaret Mary, like St. John Eudes but in her own way, to promote the spread of this devotion throughout the Church, give it definitive form, and help it to become official and universal.

Let us carefully situate the revelations she was to receive in their proper context. We have come to December 27, 1673. Margaret Mary was then twenty-six and a half years old. She had been professed for almost fourteen months. As the community's nurse's aide, insults and mishaps were daily occurrences for her in the performance of this function. Her greatest joy, when she had a few free moments, was to seek refuge before the Blessed Sacrament. On this particular day she had come as usual to be near her divine Master. The chapel is the same today as then. The altar has been replaced by another, richer and more ornate. There is also a different grille now. But we know exactly where she used to go. It was right behind the grille, as close as possible to the altar. There she would remain on her knees, very straight and motionless, in a state of intense adoration and respect.

She had come to this very place many, many times. But that particular day, the unexpected, the extraordinary, happened for her. We must let her tell us about it.

THE SAINT'S ACCOUNT

Here is her account:

"And so once, when I was before the Blessed Sacrament and had more leisure than usual, for the duties given me left me very little, I found myself surrounded by this divine presence, but so powerfully that I forgot where I was and who I was,[1] and I abandoned myself to this divine Spirit, surrendering my heart to the power of His love.

"He had me rest for a very long time on His divine breast, where He revealed to me the wonders of His love and the inexplicable secrets of His Sacred Heart, which He had always withheld from me until He *opened His heart to me for the first time,*[2] but in such an efficacious and palpable way that I no longer had any reason to doubt, because of the effects this grace produced within me, who nevertheless continue to fear I am mistaken in all that I claim is going on within me. And this, it seems to me, is how it all happened.

"He said to me:

"'My divine heart so passionately loves all men and you in particular that, no longer able to contain the flames of its burning charity, it has to pour them forth through you, and it must manifest itself to them, to enrich them with its precious treasures, which I am revealing to you, and which contain the sanctifying and salutary graces necessary to snatch them

1. These expressions leave no doubt as to the nature of this experience. It was an ecstasy.

2. Thus, she had the clear-cut impression of a revelation. However, let us not forget that this was a *private* revelation, and that the Revelation on which our faith is founded terminated with the death of the last apostle, St. John. We are not obliged to believe private revelations, but they do deserve our respect, and their purpose is to make us reflect and to nurture our devotion, providing they have been approved by the Church.

from the abyss of perdition. And I have chosen you as an abyss of unworthiness and ignorance for the fulfillment of this great plan, so that everything may be accomplished by me alone.'

"After that, He asked me to give Him my heart, which I begged Him to take, and this He did. And He placed it within His own adorable heart, in which He made me see my heart as a tiny atom being consumed in this flaming furnace, and then, drawing it out like an intense flame in the form of a heart, He put it back where He had taken it, saying to me: 'Beloved, here is a precious pledge of my love, which implants in your side a tiny spark of its most intense flames, so as to serve as your heart and consume you until your last moment, and its intensity will not die out or find refreshment except to a small degree in bloodletting, which I shall mark so completely with the blood of my cross that it will bring you more humiliation and suffering than relief. That is why I want you to ask for it simply, as much to practice what is commanded of you by the rule,[1] as to give you the consolation of shedding your blood on the cross of humiliations. And as a sign that the great grace I have just granted you *is not imaginary* and that it is the foundation of all the others I have still to give you, although I have closed the wound in your side, you will feel the pain of it forever, and although until now you have taken only the name of my slave, I now call you the beloved disciple of my Sacred Heart.'"[2]

This first revelation was still only an announcement of what was to come. Margaret Mary was to be the messenger of the Sacred Heart. She would have

1. This is an allusion to the regular practice of bloodletting, which was in use in all convents at prearranged intervals or on such occasions as it was deemed useful for an individual religious.

2. The italicizing of *is not imaginary* has been added by the present author. This does not mean that this was not going on within Margaret Mary's imagination, for it is clear that she did not see our Lord with her bodily eyes. Hers was an *imaginative* vision, but not an imaginary one. It all happened *in* her imagination but was not the product *of* her imagination. And besides, this experience was accompanied by *intellectual* lessons.

to speak in His name. She didn't know yet what she would have to say. All she had been told so far was that she had been "chosen." And to save her from any temptation to pride, Christ had added: "as an abyss of unworthiness and ignorance."

In order to understand these last words, we must remember what Margaret Mary later told Father Rolin, her Jesuit director from 1685 to 1690. The Lord had said to her: "I am seeking a victim for my heart, who is willing to sacrifice herself as a host of immolation for the fulfillment of my plans." And Margaret Mary in her humility had suggested to her divine Master "several souls who were faithfully cooperating with His plans."

But Christ had answered: "No, I want no one else but you, and that is why I have chosen you."

THE DAY AFTER THE REVELATION

What was the chosen one of the Sacred Heart going to do now? If she had been simply a visionary, an ambitious person, eager to be admired and to cause a stir, she would have hurried to publicize what had just happened to her. She did nothing of the sort. In fact, she couldn't even talk about it to her superior, as she would have wanted. She felt as though abased in her own eyes. Only the wound she felt in her side was a continual proof to her of the reality of the apparition that had been granted to her. Here is how she has described her state at this time:

"After so great a favor, and one that lasted so long, during which I didn't know if I were in heaven or on earth, I remained for several days as though completely afire and inebriated, and so much beside myself that I couldn't even say a single word except by doing myself violence. And I had to force myself so much to take recreation and eat that I found I was at the end of my strength...and this caused me extreme humiliation. And I couldn't sleep, because this wound, whose pain is so precious to me, causes me such intense fervor that it consumes me and burns me alive.[1] And I felt such a plenitude of God within me that I could not express myself to my superior as I would have wished and done, regardless of the pain and embarrassment these graces might cause me in telling about them, because of my great unworthiness, which would have made me prefer a thousand times to tell my sins to everybody. And it would have been a great consolation to me if I had been permitted to do this and to make my general confession aloud in the refectory, to show the great corruption that is in me, so that none of the graces I received would be attributed to me."

Meanwhile, Jesus was still keeping her in suspense. So far, He had only announced to her that more was to come. As always, in similar cases, He was waiting for the proper time. But every first Friday of the month, Margaret Mary would experience the reopening of the mysterious wound in her side. This was to continue until her death.

THE SECOND GREAT REVELATION

About one or two months after the great revelation of December 27, 1673, the second revelation occurred. Actually, our method of reckoning time is rather arbitrary. Margaret Mary's revelations followed each other in quick succession, growing richer each time. She intimated this herself when she wrote about the reopening of her wound each first Friday of the month:

"This Sacred Heart was shown to me as a brilliant sun of blinding light, whose burning rays fell directly on my heart, which immediately felt as though kindled by such an intense fire that it seemed

1. As always, Margaret wrote "consummate" instead of "consume." We also note that although the wound in her side was invisible, she had now become a kind of stigmatic. See the book by Dr. Biot, *L'Enigme des sigmatisés*, Paris: Bibliotheque Ecclesia, 1955.

it would reduce me to ashes. And it was especially at that time that my divine Master would teach me what He wanted of me and revealed the secrets of this loving heart."

It was probably on one of these first Fridays of the month, although we do not know the exact date, that the second great apparition took place. She has described it in a letter dated November 3, 1689, addressed to the Jesuit Father Croiset who was to write her first biography in 1691.

"This divine heart was presented to me in a throne of flames, more resplendent than a sun, transparent as crystal, with this adorable wound. *And it was surrounded with a crown of thorns,* signifying the punctures made in it by our sins, *and a cross above* signifying that from the first instant of His Incarnation, that is, as soon as the Sacred Heart was formed, the cross was implanted into it and from the first moment it was filled with all the sorrow to be inflicted on it by the humiliations, poverty, pain, and scorn His sacred humanity was to endure throughout His life and during His sacred passion.

"And He [Jesus] made me see that He intensely desired to be loved by men and to snatch them from the path of perdition onto which Satan was driving them in throngs. It was this that made Him decide to manifest His heart to men—with all the treasures of love, mercy, graces, sanctification and salvation it contained. Thus, all who wanted to render to Him and obtain for Him all the love, honor, and glory in their power would be enriched with the abundance and profusion of these divine treasures of the heart of God which was their source. This heart of God must be honored under the form of His heart of flesh, whose image He wanted exposed, and also worn on me and on my heart. He promised to pour out into the hearts of all those who honor the image of His heart all the gifts it contains in fullness, and for all those who would wear this image on their persons

[He promised] to imprint His love on their hearts and to destroy all unruly inclinations. Everywhere this holy image was exposed to be honored, He would pour forth His graces and blessings. This blessing was, as it were, a final effort of His love. He wanted to bestow upon men during these final centuries such loving redemption in order to snatch them from the control of Satan, whom He intended to destroy. He willed to place us under the sweet freedom of His rule of love, which He wanted to reestablish in the hearts of all who were willing to embrace this devotion."

In this second great revelation, our Lord began to reveal His intentions and to formulate His promises. Margaret Mary saw Him in imagination, and has described His heart surrounded with a crown of thorns with a cross above it. The Sacred Heart would henceforth be presented in this way. The image of the bleeding heart of Christ would be the symbol of His burning love for us.

This image was to be exhibited in homes or worn on the breast, especially in the form of a medal. A few years later, a nun at Paray-le-Monial made a pen drawing of the Sacred Heart with this description as a model. Margaret Mary, who by then had become mistress of novices, attached the drawing to the novitiate altar. So, in 1685, the young novices entrusted to her care were the first to venerate the image. Needless to say, the superiors' permission had been obtained to encourage the young nuns in this touching devotion.

But we have not yet come to that moment. Margaret Mary's revelations had yet to be subjected to many inquiries and much opposition.

At the time of the second great revelation of 1674, Margaret Mary was unable to tell anyone what Jesus had said to her. The time had not yet come. It was impossible—and we might add *miraculously* impossible—for her to talk to her superior about it.

She herself had no doubts at all as to the authenticity of the revelation. But in her humility she feared she might have misunderstood and thus lead others astray. So she quietly awaited her Master's further orders.

It was during the third great apparition that Christ made His will known.

THE THIRD GREAT APPARITION

Although this apparition has not been dated with certainty, we have good reason to think it took place in the beginning of June, 1674, most probably on Friday within the Octave of the Feast of Corpus Christi, for Margaret Mary has said that "the Blessed Sacrament was exposed."

Once again, let us listen to her own words:

"Once among other occasions,[1] when the Blessed Sacrament was exposed, after feeling completely drawn inward by an extraordinary recollection of all my senses and powers, Jesus Christ, my gentle Master, appeared to me resplendent with glory, with His five wounds shining like five suns, and flames issuing from every part of His sacred humanity. But above all, from His adorable breast which looked like a furnace. And uncovering His breast, He showed me His most loving and lovable heart, which was the living source of these flames. It was then that He revealed to me the inexplicable wonders of His pure love and to what excesses of love for men it had impelled Him, although He received only ingratitude and rejection from them in return.

"He said to me: 'This wounds me more than everything I suffered in my passion, since, if they returned my love in some measure I would count for little all that I have done for them, and would want, if it were possible, to do even more. But they receive all my eagerness to do them good with cold-

1. This way of speaking clearly indicates that the apparitions were frequent and revelations numerous. She has related in detail only those she considered most important.

ness and rebuffs. But give me at least the pleasure of making up for their ingratitude as much as you are able.'

"And when I showed Him how powerless I was, He answered me:

"'Take this; here is enough to make up for everything you lack!'

"And at the same time, this divine heart having burst open, such an intense flame came forth from it that I thought it would consume me, for I was so completely penetrated that I could no longer bear it and asked Him to have pity on my weakness.

"He said to me:

"'I shall be your strength; fear nothing, but be attentive to my voice and to what I ask of you, to prepare yourself to carry out my plans. First, you are to receive me in the Blessed Sacrament, as often as obedience will permit you, whatever mortifications and humiliations may come to you because of it, which you are to receive as pledges of my love. Besides, you are to receive Communion on the first Friday of each month, and during the night of Thursday to Friday I shall make you share in that mortal sadness that I willed to feel in the Garden of Olives. This sadness will reduce you, without your being able to understand it, to a kind of agony more dreadful to endure than death. To accompany me in this humble prayer that I shall then present to my Father amid all my anguish, you will rise between eleven o'clock and midnight, and prostrate yourself for one hour with me, your face against the ground, to appease the divine anger by begging mercy for sinners, and also to lessen in some manner the anguish I experienced in my abandonment by my apostles, which forced me to reproach them for not having been able to watch one hour with me. And during this hour you are to do what I shall teach you. But listen, my daughter, do not believe lightly in every spirit and do not put your trust in them, for Satan is raging to deceive you. For this reason do nothing without the approbation of those who are guiding you, so that, having the authority of obedience, you will not be deceived by him, for he has no power over the obedient.'

This time she could not escape. She had received an explicit command to tell everything to her superior, and to do nothing her God had personally commanded of her except under monastic obedience.

All this agrees so well with Catholic doctrine that we can see it only as an expression of the most authentic mysticism.

In the next chapter we shall see how she finally obtained the permissions she had been commanded to seek. And it will be clear that these permissions were not easily secured.

Let us now consider the revelation that seems to have closed the cycle for Margaret Mary. Then we shall inquire into the very important matter of how Margaret Mary succeeded in getting the episcopal authorities to recognize her apparitions as authentic. Two centuries later, Bernadette Soubirous was to face a similar problem at Lourdes.

THE LAST GREAT REVELATION

As yet, there had been no question of creating a liturgical feast in honor of the Sacred Heart. This was to be the purpose of the fourth revelation, which we can consider the last and most important of all.

The authors of the *Life of Blessed Margaret Mary*, published by the monastery of Paray-le-Monial, have written that "it would be fitting to listen on one's knees to the account of this magnificent apparition of the heart of Jesus to His servant."

This fourth major apparition occurred during the Octave of the Feast of Corpus Christi in the year 1675, that is, between June 13th and 20th. Here is Margaret Mary's account of it:

"Once when I was before the Blessed Sacrament on one of the days of its Octave, I received from my God excessive graces of His love and felt pressed to make some return and to requite love for love. He said to me:

"'You cannot requite me with greater love than by doing what I have already asked of you so many times.'"

These words imply that in the interval of a year since the previous great apparition there had been many "locutions" or calls on Christ's part to His servant. And we shall discuss in the next chapter what happened during this time.

Let us now continue Margaret Mary's account of the great apparition of June, 1675. It brings us to the most memorable part of this series of apparitions.

"Then, showing me His divine heart:

"'*Behold this heart which has so loved men* that it has spared nothing, even to the point of spending itself and being consumed to prove its love to them. And in return, I receive from most men only ingratitude because of their irreverences and sacrileges and the coldness and scorn they have for me in this Sacrament of love. But what offends me most is that hearts consecrated to me act in this way.

"'That is why I ask that the first Friday after the Octave of Corpus Christi be dedicated as a special feast to honor my heart, by receiving Holy Communion on that day and making reparation to my heart to atone for the indignities it has received ever since it has been exposed on the altars. I also promise you that my heart will dilate to pour forth in abundance the power of its divine love on those who honor it in this way and lead others to so honor it.'"

These words may be considered as the completion and crowning of the revelations addressed to our own times through the intervention of St. Margaret Mary.

We must now devote a special chapter to the verifications, discussions, contradictions, and approbations to which these apparitions and divine messages were subjected.

5

Discussions, Contradictions, and Approbations

THOSE WERE DIFFERENT TIMES

When we compare what happened in relation to the apparitions of Paray-le-Monial and what occurred at Lourdes, La Salette, or Fatima in more recent times, we note a considerable difference in the way the matters were handled.

Without going into great detail, let us take Lourdes as an example. The Blessed Virgin Mary appeared eighteen times to a little girl, ignorant but devout and pure. Almost at once the crowds began to gather. This is the habit of crowds, and such bursts of enthusiasm should always be held suspect. The clergy of Lourdes, for its part, remained cautious. But in time the evidence became unanswerable. A judgment was sought from the episcopal authority. Some years ago, Gaëtan Bernoville retraced the career of Bernadette's bishop in his book *L'Evêque de Bernadette, Mgr. Laurence.* This author laid great stress on the prudence with which Bernadette's case was examined and judged.

A commission of theologians, assisted by scholars, was set up. A canonical procedure was instituted and ran its course. After four years, on January 18, 1862, the bishop pronounced his decision in a solemn statement: "We judge that the Immaculate Mary, Mother of God, really appeared to Bernadette Soubirous on February 11, 1858, and, the following days, a total of eighteen times, in the cave of Massabielle near the city of Lourdes; that this apparition possesses all the attributes of truth and that the faithful are inclined to believe it is certain. We humbly submit our judgment to the judgment of the Sovereign Pontiff, who is charged with governing the universal Church."[1]

It can be said that such procedures have now become obligatory in the Church.

However, we shall find nothing of the sort in the case of Margaret Mary. Does this mean her apparitions were not subjected to any serious examination or verification, and that they can be rejected as doubtful, so to speak, for lack of approbation? As we shall soon see, such is not the case at all.

MARGARET MARY AND MOTHER DE SAUMAISE

For Margaret Mary, everything remained "in the family," so to speak. She had said nothing. In fact, she was unable to say anything to her superior at the time of the first great revelations and the lesser "locutions" that had occurred in the intervals between them. But during the third apparition she had received very explicit commands: to receive Communion every first Friday of the month, and to make an hour of adoration every week before the Blessed Sacrament and also during the night of Thursday preceding the first Friday. Now she was obliged to render an account to her superior. She could do nothing without her permission.

1. See M. Gaëtan Bernoville, *op. cit.* (Paris: Grasset, 1955), p. 175.

Speaking of the third great apparition, which occurred early in June, 1674, she wrote:

"And during this time, I was no longer conscious of myself and no longer knew where I was. When they came to take me away from there, seeing that I couldn't answer or even stand up without great difficulty, they led me to our Mother."

The verification was about to begin at last. A preliminary judgment would be formulated concerning the apparitions in general and that one in particular. What should Mother de Saumaise do? All she knew about the young nun could be summed up in two points: first, she had a profound esteem for her and her eminent virtues; and in the second place, she had an overly natural fear of the "extraordinary" phenomena which had already occurred in Margaret Mary—and which had delayed her profession several months.

Once more, the Mother Superior could not fail to be worried. So it was starting all over again! What was she to think of these "extraordinary ways"? They were surely not in accordance with the spirit of the Order. "Eccentricities" are always suspect in a religious community. Besides, let us picture the incident. Margaret Mary's own companions had been obliged to pick her up and drag her almost like a criminal to their superior. And then, she could hardly find words to explain what had happened to her. As she later wrote:

"For I felt like such a criminal and filled with so much shame, that no matter how harshly I might have been treated, it would have seemed too gentle to me."

Mother de Saumaise's verdict could therefore only be negative, especially before witnesses, as was most probably the case. Margaret Mary has described the scene:

"[Mother de Saumaise] finding me completely beside myself, feverish and trembling, I fell on my knees, *and then she mortified and humiliated me with all her might,* which gave me unbelievable pleasure and joy.... After having told her, although with extreme shame, what had happened, she began to humiliate me even more, *without granting me anything, for the moment, of what I thought our Lord was asking me to do,* and treating with scorn everything I had said to her. This greatly consoled me and I withdrew in a state of great peace."

And what Margaret Mary wrote, she surely believed. Her humility and obedience never left her. Besides, everyone knew the devil can masquerade as "an angel of light" and everything that had happened might just be a diabolic delusion, or false vision of some sort.

Was the whole matter to end there? If it had been a delusion, it would have been dispelled by virtue of holy obedience. For the devil dreads nothing so much as obedience, and there is nothing he so readily praises as "self-will," excessive independence, hatred of the yoke, especially the divine yoke.

Mother de Saumaise was perhaps not yet thoroughly convinced. She was even less sure when she saw the humble nun afflicted with a mysterious illness. And yet this very sickness could offer her a new reason for holding to her decision, at least for a time. Margaret Mary goes on to tell us about it:

"And the fire that was consuming me first gave me a continuous high fever, but I was too happy that I was suffering to complain about it, and I didn't tell anyone about it until my strength failed. The doctor then realized I had had this fever for a long time, and I had sixty more attacks of it afterward. I have never felt so much consolation, for with my whole body in extreme pain, this quenched to a small extent my intense thirst for suffering. This consuming fire was nurtured and content only with the wood of the cross, with all sorts of sufferings, scorn, humiliations and pain, and I never experienced any pain that could equal the pain I had from not suffering enough: it was thought I would die of it."

Then Mother de Saumaise became frightened and had a very wise idea. She said in effect to Margaret Mary:

"Why don't you ask God to cure you? In this way we'll know if all this comes from the Spirit of God. Then Communion on first Fridays, vigils on Thursday nights—I'll allow everything!"

As always, Margaret Mary obeyed.

"As I was ordered to ask our Lord to make me well, I did it, but with the fear of being answered. I was told it would be known whether all that was going on within me came from the Spirit of God by my return to health, after which I would be permitted to do what He had commanded.... Having presented all these things to our Lord, in obedience, I regained my health immediately. For the Most Blessed Virgin Mary, my good Mother, having favored me with her presence, embraced me tenderly, and told me after a rather long conversation:

"'Take courage, my dear daughter, in the health I give you in the name of my divine Son, for you have still a long and painful road to travel, always bearing the cross, pierced with nails and thorns and lacerated by whips. But have no fear, I shall not abandon you and I promise to protect you.'

"This is a promise she has made me feel very keenly since then, in the great need I have had of it."

She was making some headway. The mother superior of the monastery was giving in. That was still very little, but it was a beginning.

THE THEOLOGICAL CONSULTATION

Mother de Saumaise continued to wonder. Following the most authentic spirit of the Church, she decided to consult theologians. Margaret Mary was the first to want it, fearing she had been mistaken and might deceive others—a fear that persisted until she died.

According to the *Life by the Contemporaries,* Mother de Saumaise, "hesitating to lead her by these eminent paths of perfection where God was calling her, thought she should require her to break the deep silence she had kept until then and speak to a few persons learned in matters of doctrine, to whom she was to reveal what was going on within her."

A DIVINE INTERVENTION

At her superior's command, therefore, Margaret Mary appeared before "persons of doctrine" of whom we know nothing, not even their names. She was obliged to tell these venerable personages everything that had happened to her. We readily guess she did this only with extreme timidity. Opinions were divided on her case.

The *Life by the Contemporaries* says: "God permitted, to increase His servant's merit, that *a few* of those whom she consulted did not at first recognize the Spirit that guided her. They condemned her great attraction to mental prayer, called her a visionary, and forbade her to pay any attention to her inspirations." It even says that one of the counselors who had been invited to express an opinion had casually answered: "Give this girl some soup to eat and everything will be better."

The wisest of the counselors suspended judgment. But neither Mother de Saumaise nor Margaret could find much reassurance in this consultation.

Meanwhile, Margaret, obedient as ever, did her best to fight off her inspirations:

"I made every effort to resist these attractions, believing I was surely in error. But as I couldn't overcome them I had no doubt I was abandoned, since I was being told it was not the Spirit of God who was governing me and nonetheless it was impossible for me to resist this Spirit."

HELP FROM HEAVEN

In the darkness that surrounded her, she still had only one refuge: the divine heart that had been revealed to her. So she came to her divine Master with her most recent troubles. He answered that He would soon send her His "faithful servant," to whom He wanted her to tell her story when the time came, and to whom she was to entrust the treasures of His heart, because he was being sent to strengthen her in her mission.

Who was this faithful servant? Margaret Mary had no idea, and no one else seemed to know. It is quite certain that the tribunal of "persons of doctrine" before whom she had been forced to appear included all the notables among the local clergy. In particular, it must have included the Jesuit Superior, Father R.P. Papon. Now, he hadn't understood the saint either. A very energetic, zealous man, frank to the point of rudeness, it has been said of him that "he was better qualified to unscramble the consciences of merchants and soldiers than of cloistered nuns."[1]

And yet it was from the local Jesuit residence that Margaret Mary was to receive the help promised by the Lord. Early in 1675, Father Papon was transferred to the school at Gray, as headmaster. His provincial at the time was the famous Father de la Chaize, later to be the confessor of King Louis XIV. It is possible, even probable, that Father Papon told his provincial about the happenings at Paray-le-Monial. This was to weigh heavily in the provincial's choice of a successor for Father Papon.

As Providence would have it, Father de la Chaize found just the right man near at hand. For almost four years he had followed the progress of a young Jesuit named Claude La Colombière, who was thirty-four years old in 1675. He was one of the hopes of

1. These lines were written by G. Guitton, S.J., in his beautiful biography, *Le Bienheureux Claude La Colombière* (Paris, 1943), p. 235. In what follows, we are using this definitive work as our source.

the Society of Jesus in France, cultured, brilliant, and also a pious man. The story is told that when a lady under his direction, Marie Rosalie de Lyonne, expressed surprise that a man such as he had been assigned to such an insignificant town as Paray-le-Monial, Father Forest, of Paray-le-Monial, is said to have answered: "It is for the benefit of a chosen soul who needs his guidance."

A chosen soul! This was indeed the case. And such souls weigh heavily in the mystical scales of God. Margaret Mary had a great future, and she was in great distress before the arrival of this "faithful servant" of her God!

"They began to tell me that the devil was the author of all that was happening within me and that he would destroy me, if I were not careful, by his deceits and delusions."

Exactly the same thing had happened a hundred years earlier to Teresa of Avila. In her case, too, there were endless consultations. Even the most confident doctors seemed paralyzed and hesitant. And it had required no less than the greatest theologians of Spain, not to mention great saints like Peter of Alcantara and Francis Borgia, to begin to understand what was going on.

FATHER LA COLOMBIÈRE

Seven or eight months had now elapsed since the great apparition of early June, 1674, which had aroused such controversy over Margaret Mary's case. In February, 1675, the new Jesuit superior at Paray-le-Monial, Father La Colombière, made his first visit to the Visitation. Like his predecessor Father Papon, he was to be the nuns' "extraordinary confessor." He was introduced to the community, and gave a short allocution. Margaret Mary understood at once what was happening to her.

"I heard inwardly the words: '*Here is the one I am sending you.*' And I soon realized this during my ember day confession."

We should note in passing that the "extraordinary confessor" came to hear confessions only during ember days. That year, the ember days of Lent occurred on March 6th, 8th, and 9th.

Let no one suppose that Margaret Mary hastened to make all sorts of disclosures to the new confessor, although the Lord had inwardly informed her that He had sent him to her. She would never "climb over Providence," to use an expression coined by St. Vincent de Paul. And yet Father La Colombière made her feel at ease from the start, and made her understand he had heard many things, either from the mother superior, his predecessor Father Papon, or from general gossip.

"Although we had never seen or spoken to each other before, he kept me for a very long time and talked to me as if he understood what was going on within me. But I did not choose to open my heart to him on that occasion. And as he saw that I wanted to leave for fear of inconveniencing the community, he told me that if I agreed he would come and see me at another time, to talk with me in this same place. But my natural timidity, which made me fear all these communications, led me to answer him that, since I was not my own, I would do everything obedience commanded. I left after remaining there about an hour and a half."

Such was their first interview, and Margaret Mary's deeply significant answer. For a Jesuit, her reserve, her determination to talk freely only "under orders" and under cover of "holy obedience," were most reassuring. For to a Jesuit, obedience held first place among the virtues of a religious. He already had all the proof he needed.

However, in the confessional he had not seen the young nun. We can well surmise that he continued to keep this matter in mind and that in prayer he was preparing himself to do whatever God would command him in Margaret Mary's regard.

In any event, Mother de Saumaise soon invited him to give a spiritual conference to the nuns. This time it was in the chapel, and the black grille curtain had been drawn, as was the custom. Father La Colombière spoke from the wicket-gate used to give Communion, but he could see his audience through the choir grille. Among the nuns present he noticed one "in whom he discerned something extraordinary." Her outward recollection revealed what was going on within her. She made such an impression on him that after his conference he felt obliged to ask the mother superior who this young nun was.

When Mother de Saumaise told him it was Margaret Mary, he quickly replied: "That is a soul of grace!"

This was enough to reassure the superior, who was still considerably worried about the young sister. She decided to consult this Jesuit, who had already attained some fame. She also commanded her daughter to hide nothing from him.

He returned to the Visitation, probably in mid-March, 1675. Margaret Mary was well prepared both by her private revelations and by the explicit commands of her superior. Even so, she experienced "frightful reticence" in speaking to him. This sentiment was so strong that the first thing she did was to tell him so. The priest answered: "I am very glad to have given you an opportunity to make a sacrifice to God."

MARGARET MARY TELLS ALL

"Without hesitation or ceremony I opened my soul to him as well as I could. He gave me great consolations concerning myself, assuring me that there was nothing to fear in the guidance of this Spirit, *inasmuch as He was not turning me away from obedience;* and that I should obey His inspirations, abandoning my whole being to Him, to sacrifice and immolate myself according to His good pleasure.

Admiring the great mercy of our God, for not being disgusted with such resistance, he taught me to value God's gifts and to accept with respect and humility the frequent and intimate conversations with which He favored me, for which I should continually give thanks."

This made a great deal of sense. A "spirit" that inspires perfect "obedience," that leaves one in complete humility, in peace and joy, is surely a spirit that comes from God. But once it was agreed that "all that" came from God, then it should be accepted with the greatest respect, with continual thanksgiving! It had to be all or nothing. Either everything had to be rejected with contempt, or everything was to be welcomed with transports of joy!

Now that the promised "faithful servant" had come and she had consulted with him, Margaret Mary was truly happy. Indeed, all her struggles were not yet over. They would end only with death, and arguments were to rage over her revelations long after her death. But she could see where she was going now, and she went ahead in obedience and joy. However, like all her other joys, God's will would permit this one to be clouded by suffering.

Opposition had not yet ceased within the community. Divisions arose among the nuns concerning Margaret Mary. And this cost her "many humiliations," as she herself later said. What troubled her most was that Father La Colombière was not spared either. She had declared that he "had much to suffer" on her account "because it was said I wanted to deceive him by my delusions and to mislead him like the others."

These were inevitable squabbles, such as Teresa of Avila had also experienced a century earlier. For the time being, Father La Colombière knew nothing of these pinpricks and murmurs. In fact, a few weeks before Easter he left Paray-le-Monial to preach a mission elsewhere.

But he returned to Paray before the end of Lent, and we can be sure one of the first things he did was to visit the Monastery of the Visitation.

INCREASED OPPOSITION

It was high time he returned to encourage poor Margaret Mary. Opposition was growing around her. As could be expected in a convent where silence is the rule, this animosity found expression most of the day in the form of meaningful headshakes, reproving glances, surly faces. Having a visionary in the house, according to some nuns, was like an invasion from the devil himself. It was a danger, a threat to everyone. It went so far that Margaret Mary later admitted that some of the sisters used to "throw holy water" on her, as though to exorcise Satan's obsession from her.

This is no exaggeration on our part. Authentic documentation exists on this sort of incomprehension of our saint. She prayed for humiliations, and she received them in abundance. And they came every day, in spite of her perfect obedience to all the requirements of the holy rule.

At the beatification process which took place in 1715, twenty-five years after her death, the nuns who had known her made depositions under oath. We know what they have declared. Many of them agreed with what Sister Damas de Barnay said, for instance:

"That she happened on several occasions to be present during the recreations where the aforementioned Sister Alacoque, also present, was called a visionary, a hypocrite, obstinate in her sentiments and devotions."

And Sister Rosselin in her turn affirmed "she knew that the aforementioned Sister Alacoque suffered all it is possible to suffer of contempt, contradictions, rebuffs, insults, and reproaches, without complaining."

Then, too, Sister Claudia Margaret Billet reports that on one occasion she was "with her while others, at a distance, made a point of talking loudly as they blamed and reviled her cruelly. She [Margaret Mary] told the deposing sister who wanted to lead her away so she would not hear this evil talk: 'My dear sister, if only you knew how sweet it is to suffer for Jesus Christ!'"

Actually, these depositions do not refer solely to the period extending from the third to the fourth great apparition, from June, 1674 to June, 1675.

At first, the members of the community knew very little of what had happened in the convent chapel between the young professed nun and our Lord. But they knew something had happened. They also knew that Margaret Mary had to be taken to the superior, Mother de Saumaise, after the third apparition. And on that occasion she had been seen to stammer and blush. The severe reprimand by the mother superior had been remembered.

It was also known, of course, that in the end Margaret Mary had obtained what she had asked, namely, Communion on the first Fridays of the month and the holy hour every week. And for many nuns who had been at Paray-le-Monial much longer than she, such things seemed very strange, eccentric, some sort of a fad!

This opposition, which we have merely sketched, was to continue for several more years. So we can see that Margaret Mary needed all the understanding Father La Colombière could give her.

FATHER LA COLOMBIÈRE'S COURAGE

Father La Colombière needed genuine courage to hold fast to the position he had taken. Was he not risking his reputation for wisdom and prudence? Might not his apostolate be endangered by the lively arguments around Margaret Mary? She, too, was aware of the situation. She has written about it:

"I was amazed a hundred times that he did not abandon me the way the others had done; for the way I talked with him would have disgusted anyone else."

Father La Colombière for his part went ahead with an assurance that nothing could deter. One of the earliest resolves he had made as a religious was never to be influenced by human judgments. As a young Jesuit he had written: "I don't want to be a success in the eyes of men." The more he studied the problem presented by Margaret Mary, the more clearly did he discern God's will.

There were reasons of principle and reasons of practical fact to consider. The reasons of principle were based on the theological soundness of devotion to the Sacred Heart. Without going into all the signs of this devotion over the centuries, either in St. Gertrude, or in an unknown Carthusian monk named John Justin Lansperge, Father La Colombière had learned precious lessons on this holy devotion from the Jesuit Father Nouet.

However, that was not sufficient to make him believe this unknown nun had received revelations and explicit instructions from the Sacred Heart Himself. But with regard to this current aspect of the question, he had good reasons to declare he was in favor of accepting the apparitions as real. It was Margaret Mary's spirit of obedience that had impressed and won him, as he had clearly witnessed it firsthand. To the end, this is the point to which he would give the greatest importance.

A few years later, after his return from England and when he was already a very sick man, he wrote from Lyons to Mother de Saumaise, who was no longer at Paray either:

"I have been able to see Sister à la Coque [sic] only once, but I was greatly consoled by this visit [to Paray]; I find her, as always, extemely humble, obedient, with a great love for the cross and for humiliation. These are marks of the goodness of the spirit that leads her, and have never misled anyone."

These lines deserve serious meditation. They give us a striking example of the "discernment of spirits" according to St. Ignatius. The devil is capable of doing many things, but he will never, never inspire humility, obedience, love for the cross—in a word, love for our Lord Jesus Christ!

Apart from these reasons, did Father La Colombière have still others that were more "current," more personal? In short, did he have reasons that cannot be given because they go beyond all human understanding and definitely belong to the supernatural order? It seems that he did indeed have such reasons. It was not he who told us about them, but Margaret Mary herself, in the following passage concerning an incident that occurred one morning when he came to celebrate Mass at the Visitation during this year of 1675.

"Our Lord granted very great graces to him, and to me, too. For, when I came up to receive Holy Communion, He showed me His Sacred Heart as a blazing furnace, and two other hearts being swallowed up in it, and He said to me: 'Behold, how my pure love unites these three hearts forever.'"

What she understood of this vision was that her union to Father La Colombière was "all for the glory of the Sacred Heart." But she also understood she had to tell her director about it. "[Our Lord] wanted me to reveal to him the treasures of this heart, so that he might make them known and proclaim their worth and usefulness."

And she concluded:

"To this end, [our Lord] wanted us to be as brother and sister, sharing His spiritual riches equally."

What was happening at the same time in the Jesuit's saintly soul? He has not made it known. But, being prudent and wise, it is certain he would never have agreed to such spiritual intimacy if it had not responded to his own private inspirations.

Margaret Mary apologized for her boldness. She protested "her poverty and the inequality existing between a man of such great virtue and a miserable sinner like herself." But her Jesus answered: "The infinite riches of my heart will make up for all that and equalize everything. Just *tell him,* without fear!"

So she obeyed. She told Father La Colombière everything. And we surmise he discovered what the holy nun was telling him echoed his own deepest aspirations. As proof of this, we cite the following passage.

"[Since Jesus had commanded: 'Just tell him!'], that is what I did at our first interview. I was touched by the humble manner and gratitude with which he listened to this, as well as several other things I told him in the name of my sovereign Master, about himself...and this was more helpful to me than all the sermons I could have heard."

THE GREAT REVELATION AND THE OBLATION OF REPARATION

We come now to the last great revelation to Margaret Mary, the one relating to the creation of a feast in honor of the Sacred Heart. Father La Colombière, without even realizing it, was to become its principal exponent.

He had commanded Margaret Mary "to write what was going on within her." This meant that he was taking the matter very seriously and wanted to be able to meditate upon it at leisure. But, as she admitted, the very thought of writing filled her with "a mortal repugnance." And she added: "I would write in obedience, and then I would burn [what I had written], thinking I had adequately fulfilled the demands of obedience." If we understand her correctly, she burned her writings without showing them to Father La Colombière. But that could not suffice! It caused her some twinges of conscience. In the end, she was explicitly forbidden to burn what she wrote.

The fourth and last great revelation occurred soon afterwards. In obedience to her spiritual director, she set it all down in writing. When Father La Colombière's superiors subsequently assigned him to England, he took Margaret Mary's writings with him. While in London, he wrote out a Retreat in January, 1677. Without telling Margaret Mary, he inserted her account of the fourth revelation at the end of his own manuscript.

Shortly after Father La Colombière's death in 1682, his Retreat, with Margaret Mary's account at the end, was published. It found a wide audience. This was to be the first step toward the execution of Christ's command to Margaret Mary to promote the institution of a feast in honor of His Sacred Heart throughout the Church.

Actually, it had been foretold. After the great revelation in which Jesus called for a feast in honor of His Sacred Heart,[1] Margaret Mary had said to Him:

"But my Lord, whom are You asking? A puny creature and a poor sinner, whose very unworthiness could prevent the execution of Your plan. You have so many generous souls to carry out Your wishes."

Jesus had answered:

"'Well! Poor innocent [sic] that you are, don't you know that I make use of the weakest to confound the strong, that it is usually the most lowly and the poor in spirit on whom I make my power shine forth most brightly so they may not claim any credit for themselves?'

'Pray, give me the means to do what You command,' I said.

"Then He added: 'Speak to my servant...and tell him from me to do what he can to establish this devotion and give my divine heart this pleasure; he must not be discouraged by the obstacles he will encounter, for there will be many, but he must know

1. See page 91 above, dealing with this revelation.

that he who doesn't put his trust in himself but puts all his trust in me, such a one is all-powerful.'"

We know that Father La Colombière was so impressed with the message, and also by what concerned him personally in it, that he wanted to be the first to do what the Sacred Heart had commanded: To make amends to Him by a reparation of honor. He received Communion that very day in reparation for the indignities the Sacred Heart had received throughout the time the Host had been exposed on the altars.

In 1675, the Octave of Corpus Christi ended on June 20th. The next day, June 21st, he made the act of reparation. This form of reparation was to be one of the essential aspects of devotion to the Sacred Heart as understood by Margaret Mary. It was simpler, easier to understand and more popular than the lofty, theological approach of St. John Eudes.

REPARATION OF HONOR

The term "reparation of honor" was part of the judicial vocabulary of the time. Old French law understood it to mean a humiliating punishment, suffered in reparation. For example, the public confession of a crime with a plea to society for forgiveness.

Father La Colombière was then the only person who had read Margaret Mary's account of her last great revelation. What was he going to do about it? He no longer had any doubts as to the divine origin of the Spirit that was guiding her. He certainly must have commanded Margaret Mary to make this reparation of honor requested by our Lord. But he did more. He wanted to perform the same act he was requiring of the humble nun. This is how the matter is described in the *Life by the Contemporaries*, written after Margaret Mary's death.

"Father La Colombière, who had very sound judgment, was not a man to believe anything lightly; but he had too startling proofs of the solid virtue of the person speaking to him to fear the slightest delusion in this matter. That is why he immediately dedicated himself to the ministry that God had entrusted to him. And in order to carry it out reliably and perfectly, he decided to begin with himself. He therefore consecrated himself totally to the Sacred Heart of Jesus, offering everything there might be in him that could honor and please the Sacred Heart. This consecration took place on Friday, June 21, 1675. It was the day after the Octave of Corpus Christi, and can be regarded as the date when devotion to the Sacred Heart made its first conquest."

Actually, Father Guitton, one of the modern biographers of Blessed Claude La Colombière, does not think the priest consecrated himself in the strict sense of the word on that day. He is convinced, and we agree with him, that Father La Colombière, always so cautious and meticulous, did not exceed the limits of what was asked of him. This is what Father Guitton has to say:

"When it is affirmed that Blessed La Colombière 'consecrated himself' to the Sacred Heart as early as June 21, 1675, no one can object so long as nothing more is implied than this reparation of honor....

"That Claude later offered himself totally to the heart of Jesus—consecration in the strict sense—is certain. At the end of his *Journal of Retreats*, we find references both to the motives that led him to make it and the formula he used in his act of oblation. But did he make it, and in these very words, as early as the month of June, 1675?"

Father Guitton has serious doubts about this, and it would seem his doubts are justified. Things did not move as fast as we might be tempted to believe.

Ten years were to elapse before the Feast of the Sacred Heart was adopted even by the monastery of Paray, and this was done because Father La Colombière had suggested it. The first celebration of the feast took place in 1685, three years after Father La Colombière's death.

TEN YEARS LATER

Throughout those ten years, conflict had persisted around the case of Margaret Mary. In 1678, Mother de Saumaise, who had protected and admired her, left the monastery [of Paray to become superior at Moulins]. She was succeeded by Mother Greyfié, who took a much sterner attitude toward the young saint.

Previously, on November 20, 1677, there had been a terrifying scene. At the repeated commands of her Lord and of Mother de Saumaise, who was then very ill, Margaret Mary delivered a message to the community. More dead than alive, the young nun stood up before the community and told them of the "punishments that divine justice" intended to inflict on that very monastery.

Margaret Mary's first biographer, Father Croiset, has related the incident, as remembered by some of the survivors who had witnessed it. The messenger of Christ knelt motionless, "in the midst of these mutinous and riotous girls." This is how Margaret Mary described it in her *Autobiography:*

"If I had been able to gather together all the sufferings I had experienced until then and all those I have had since, and if all of them had continued until death, this would not seem comparable to me to what I endured that night!"

And she added these words, which Father Guitton feels should be taken quite literally:

"I was dragged from one place to another, with unbelievable humiliations."

This had been the culminating moment of opposition against her. Most of the nuns opposing her quickly realized they had gone too far. The next morning, November 21st, "there were not enough confessors" to meet the needs of all the nuns seeking absolution. During Mass on that day, Margaret Mary had the consolation of hearing the following words deep within her soul:

"Finally, peace has been established and my holiness of justice is satisfied by the sacrifice you have made to me!"

However, there still remained a kind of distrust for Margaret Mary's revelations.

It was only when Mother Melin became superior that the first steps were made toward establishing devotion to the Sacred Heart. Mother Melin had formerly been a member of the community at Paray, and knew Margaret Mary very well. Much against her will, Margaret Mary was named assistant to the superior.

As we have already mentioned, Father La Colombière died in 1682, and his *Spiritual Retreat* was published soon afterward. Sometime after July, 1685, this book was read in the refectory at Paray-le-Monial.[1]

Now, Margaret Mary was not only assistant, but also mistress of novices. In honor of the feast of St. Margaret, the young novices decided to honor the Sacred Heart, knowing that nothing could please their mistress more. But when one of them went to invite the professed nuns to share in this celebration, she was mortified at the answer she received from Sister Mary Magdalene des Escures, one of the most energetic and well-meaning nuns of the community:

"Go and tell your mistress that sound devotion is the practice of our Rules and Constitutions, and this is what she is supposed to teach you, and what you are to practice diligently."

This sharp answer gives us an idea of the serious reasons and even justification for the opposition to any new devotion. But something was going to happen that would put an end to all this opposition.

1. Although Father Guitton cites this date in his book (p. 660), M. Hamon, in his biography of St. Margaret Mary, situated this incident during the first months of 1685.

The nun in charge of choosing the material to be read in the refectory had apparently neglected to read Father La Colombière's book beforehand, for everyone assumed it would be reliable, pious, and edifying. They were coming to the end of his book, and had reached a very stirring passage on Eucharistic devotion. The author wrote that when he was before the Holy Eucharist "my heart overflows and feels joys that I experience and receive from my God, without being able to explain them.... You are most merciful, my God, to give Yourself to this most ungrateful of creatures and unworthiest of servants; I shall praise and bless You for it eternally."

Who can doubt the effect these words had upon the hearts of all the nuns, and Margaret Mary in particular? She must surely have adored the divine Captive of the Eucharist in union with the deceased priest who had helped her so much ten years earlier, and who had become her "brother" before God!

The reader continued. Without any transition, she came to the passage which rang out in the deepening silence.

As the nuns listened attentively, this is what they heard:

"I realized that God wanted me to serve Him by carrying out His wishes concerning the devotion He had recommended to a person to whom He reveals Himself very freely, and for whose sake He has deigned to make use of my weakness."

A devotion? Did we understand correctly? A devotion recommended to a person to whom He reveals Himself freely? Who could this person be? One of the novices, Sister Claudia Rosalie Farges, could not refrain from glancing at her mistress, although this was against refectory rules. At the beatification process of 1715, she was to declare that she had caught a furtive glimpse of Margaret Mary "lowering her eyes in deep self-abasement."

The reader continued. Now she was reading Margaret Mary's own account of the last great revelation of June, 1675, written at the explicit command of Father La Colombière. There it was, all printed in his book.

Excitement spread from one nun to the next throughout the refectory. Everyone was silent. They continued to eat, as if nothing out of the ordinary had happened. But they all felt intense curiosity about the book whose contents were unknown to them. Although she had not been mentioned by name in the book, Margaret Mary was recognized by all the nuns as the "person" referred to. She was on burning coals. We can assume that the reader was unable to read this passage aloud without some tremors of emotion:

"And so: God having manifested Himself to this person (who we have reason to believe is according to His heart because of the great graces He has granted her), she told me about it and I made her put in writing what she had said. And this I have wanted to describe in the journal of my retreats, because the good God wants to use my weak capacities to put this plan into effect."

Then followed the entire account of the fourth revelation as we already know it. There could be no mistake. The "person" according to God's heart, everyone felt, could only be Sister Alacoque. Yes, it was she! And her adversaries had not known the details of the great secret she had guarded so carefully for ten long years. And even less did they know that she had entrusted her secret to one man, a priest and a holy religious, a theologian and a saint, namely, Father La Colombière. Now he was revealing it for all to know, with his most enthusiastic approbation. He had made Margaret Mary's message his own, going so far as to comply with its demands. He wanted to devote what he called his "weak capacities" to work for the institution of a feast in honor of the Sacred Heart.

At the recreation which followed, the novice—that *enfant terrible* who had furtively looked up during the meal—came to her mother mistress and said: "My dear Sister, your story was told today, and Father La Colombière could not have pointed more clearly to you."

The mistress of novices simply answered, according to Sister Farges, "that she had good reason to love her abjection."

A great step forward had been made. Now that our saint had the support of such a wise and holy priest, she could begin her apostolate. She had waited ten years for her hour! At last, public devotion to the Sacred Heart, as she had been commanded to propagate it, would soon spread by leaps and bounds.

In the next chapter we shall tell about this development, as it occurred during Margaret Mary's lifetime, until her death in 1690.

6

Nature and Expansion of Devotion to the Sacred Heart, According to Margaret Mary

MARGARET MARY'S MISSION

Margaret Mary's apparitions were not granted to her for her own benefit. They were addressed to the entire Catholic world. In the four great apparitions that we have enumerated and described, there was a clear-cut progression from one to the other.

In the first apparition, Jesus told His servant that He had chosen her to propagate devotion to His heart, but He did not yet request any specific form of devotion to the Sacred Heart. In the second apparition, He showed her His heart surrounded by thorns and surmounted with a cross. And He made her clearly understand that devotion to His divine heart was to be a worship of reparation. This was to be one of the essential marks of the devotion to the Sacred Heart originating at Paray-le-Monial. We have still to explain the theological importance and depth of this aspect of reparation.

In the third apparition, Jesus asked His servant to promote the practice of receiving Holy Communion on the first Friday of each month, and the practice of a holy hour before the Blessed Sacrament during the night of Thursday to Friday. Finally, in the fourth apparition, He requested that a liturgical feast in honor of the Sacred Heart be instituted in the Church. This feast was to be celebrated on the Friday after the end of the Octave of Corpus Christi.

It is easy to discern what new elements Margaret Mary brought to the devotion to the Sacred Heart as it had been practiced by many saints and devout persons before her, and as it was already beginning to be practiced in public in the communities founded by St. John Eudes, or in the Congregation of Calvary founded by the well-known Father Joseph.

In the first place, Margaret Mary was directly instructed by her Lord and Master, Jesus Christ. She did not invent anything out of her own fertile mind, nor did she deduce anything from theological speculation. In the second place, the lessons she learned from her Jesus tended to simplify and clarify the very object of this devotion.

In 1672, that is, before Margaret Mary's first great apparition, a feast in honor of the Sacred Heart had been approved by the bishops of Normandy. This was at the request of St. John Eudes, the most famous apostle of the Sacred Heart at that time, and he obtained it only for his own communities of men and women. He explained devotion to the Sacred Heart in a more scholarly and less popular way:

"It embraces at once the fleshly heart of the God-Man, His spiritual heart, and His divine heart.... Three hearts that are but one, because His divine heart is the soul, the heart and the life of His spiritual and fleshly heart. And they are joined in such perfect unity in Him that these three hearts are but one; they are one single heart, filled with infinite love for the Most Blessed Trinity and with unimaginable charity for men."

In the above passage, St. John Eudes defined the "spiritual heart" as "the superior part of His sacred soul, which includes His memory, His understanding, and His will."

All this was indeed very beautiful, but perhaps a bit too complicated for ordinary Christians. It is not surprising, therefore, that Margaret Mary was called to simplify this very lofty theology. For the devotion she was commanded to spread was addressed to all Catholics everywhere. She drew attention first of all to Christ's fleshly heart. The image of the heart crowned with thorns and surmounted with a cross is very eloquent. For in every land and in every language, the heart is the symbol of love. Now, the devotion emanating from Paray-le-Monial certainly does not exclude uncreated love—what John Eudes calls the "divine heart"—that is, the love with which the Word Incarnate loves inasmuch as He is God. And yet, this devotion focuses above all on created love, that is, on what John Eudes calls the "spiritual heart" of Christ, by which the Word Incarnate loves in His human nature.

It is also very important to note that the devotion of Paray stresses the idea of atonement and reparation of honor. And what does this mean? We must insist on this point.

THE MYSTICAL SCALES

The whole Christian religion rests on the idea of satisfaction and reparation. The God-Man has paid the debts of all men. The Son of Man has made amends for Adam, the Father of men, and all his descendants.

There is a kind of *mystical scales* in which all human actions are weighed. In one of the trays are held all the sins of the universe, to which each of us has contributed his or her share. But in the other tray, Christ has placed His sufferings, His passion, His blood, His supreme sacrifice.

As Catholics we believe that a single drop of this divine blood has greater worth before God than all the sins of the human race. We believe that this universal debt of the human race has been paid. We believe that by means of the sacraments instituted by Christ and administered by His Church, we can apply to ourselves the merits and graces that our Redeemer has won. The very title of Redeemer, Savior, that we give Him is an affirmation of our faith.

However, we also know that Christ generously allows those who love Him to share in His cross. Their sufferings, their labors, their good works, all their merits, in short, are added to the satisfactions of Christ. St. Paul did not hesitate to say: "I find my joy in the suffering I endure for you. In my own flesh I fill up what is lacking in the sufferings of Christ for the sake of his body, the church" (1 Col. 1:24).

The sufferings of the friends of Jesus are more of Jesus' own sufferings. Paul knew it better than anyone, for had he not heard Christ say to him on the road to Damascus: "Saul, Saul, why do you persecute me?" (Acts 9:4) When the disciples of Jesus are persecuted, Jesus Himself is persecuted. It would be easy to give endless examples of reparation. And this idea, so essential to the Christian religion that it is its very heart, is precisely the idea of the devotion to the Sacred Heart as revealed in the apparitions and locutions granted to Margaret Mary.

It is perhaps less well known that this idea, in an archaic form, made its appearance in the earliest times. Take, for instance, the eighteenth chapter of Genesis, which deals with the terrible punishment in store for the cities of Sodom and Gomorrah. Abraham begged mercy for the two sinful cities. He asked God if fifty good men in the city could hold back the arm of divine justice. And from fifty he went down to forty-five, then to forty, thirty, twenty, and finally ten. And Yahweh said to him: "For the sake of those ten, I will not destroy it" (Gen. 18:32).

Unfortunately, there weren't even ten just men to be found.

In this very ancient story we clearly discern the notion of the mystical scales. The just save the world.

As the unknown author of the beautiful *Letter to Diognetus* wrote in the second century A.D., Christians are "to the world what the soul is to the body."

As members of the Mystical Body of Christ, we have a world-wide function to fulfill. In union with Jesus, we make reparation, we offer God the satisfaction His justice demands, so that the world may live and retain its reason for being.

This is the idea the Church has chosen to emphasize in Margaret Mary's message. In the end, it was this doctrine that led to the institution of a special feast in honor of the Sacred Heart and the practice of Holy Hours before the Blessed Sacrament as well as First Friday Communions. In his Encyclical *Miserentissimus Redemptor*, Pope Pius XI has clearly made this point:

"When Christ appeared to Margaret Mary and revealed His infinite charity to her, He also let her perceive a kind of sadness in Him in His complaints against the countless and grievous insults He suffered by reason of men's ingratitude. May the words He then spoke become firmly engraved in the souls of the faithful and never be erased!"

Then he declared that one of our principal duties toward the heart of Jesus was the "reparation of honor," which he called a duty "in justice and love." Why? Because "compensations are due to uncreated Love for the injustice inflicted upon it by neglect and indifference or by offenses committed against it."

Finally, the Pope instituted and made obligatory a reparation of honor on the Feast of the Sacred Heart, "so that we might deplore all our sins and make reparation to the outraged rights of Christ, our sovereign King and most loving Lord."

There can be no doubt, therefore, as to the profound Catholicity of devotion to the Sacred Heart as it was recommended to Margaret Mary by her divine Lord.

This is all the more evident inasmuch as she was totally devoid of theological training in the strict sense. Let us now consider how she succeeded in carrying out the commands she had received from Christ.

ACTS OF REPARATION NECESSARY

Margaret Mary did not know, and she might have died of grief and shame if she had, that Paris, the capital of her beloved France, was then the scene of obscene profanations. And this under the glorious King Louis XIV! All the historians of our saint have pointed this out. We need not, therefore, discuss it in detail here.

Suffice it to mention a few names. There were the Marquise of Brinvilliers and her accomplice, the Voisin woman, both convicted and burned to death as poisoners. There was the special tribunal created to deal with crimes, in which persons of the highest nobility and even a marshal of France were implicated. Then there were the shocking profanations to which the Blessed Sacrament of the Eucharist was being subjected. Indeed, Louis Bourdaloue, the famous Jesuit preacher, did not hesitate to speak of it before the king and his entire court, in his sermon on impurity:

"Would anyone have believed that sacrilege might become the seasoning of a brutish passion?... That what is most venerable in religion should be used for what is most corrupt in debauchery and that man, in fulfillment of Isaiah's prophecy, uses his God even for his most sordid lusts?"

Now, it was precisely at this epoch that Jesus was pressing His devout servant with His holy demands and asking her to "make reparation" for sinners! We have two kinds of documents that explain how she did in fact perform acts of reparation. On the one hand, we have her *Autobiography* written from 1685 to 1687 at the command of her then spiritual director,

Father Rolin. And on the other hand, we have the collection of her letters, extending from 1678 until 1690, the year of her death.

There is an amazing contrast between these two sources of information. In the *Autobiography* where she was under obedience to tell all, we come across continual references to sufferings, humiliations, and trials beyond counting. It seems this holy nun was continually being afflicted, tormented, indeed crushed, and that in addition she overcame her natural revulsions to the point of zealously practicing every sort of mortification and penance, even some that are all but impossible to describe.

In her letters, on the other hand, Margaret Mary always wrote with a gentleness, a delicate tenderness, a calm and peace that might have indicated her life was unfolding in perfect tranquillity and amid unclouded joy. True, she always referred to herself as a very "puny creature," as a poor "sinner," who had great need of "conversion." But as she gave no details, these expressions could be taken as a matter of style or as acts of voluntary humility. Actually, she herself has admitted, she was simply obeying Jesus:

"This sovereign Spirit that operated and acted in me independently of me, had seized such absolute control over my whole spiritual and even bodily being that it was no longer in my power to command any feeling of joy or sadness except at His good pleasure; nor could I focus my mind on anything except what He presented to it."

MARGARET MARY'S LETTERS

The passage we have just quoted is taken from the *Autobiography*. But now we shall turn to the collection of her letters, and choose passages from some of the most beautiful.

Many of her letters, in fact the most beautiful, were addressed to her dear Mother de Saumaise, either at Moulins, where the latter was superior from 1678 to 1681, or at Dijon, where she went subsequently.

What did Margaret Mary say in these letters? The following lines give us some idea:

"Truthfully, my dear Mother, I don't know what to say to those I love, unless I speak to them of the cross of Jesus Christ, and when I am asked what graces our Lord grants me, an unworthy sinner, I can only speak of the happiness there is in suffering with Jesus Christ, for I see nothing more precious in this life, for those who love Him, than to suffer for love of Him."

In a letter dated January 20, 1682, to the same mother, she gives the following details:

"...He placed three persecutors in my soul which tormented me continually. The first, that produced the two others, is such a great desire to love Him that it seems everything I see ought to be transformed into flames of love, so that He may be loved in His divine Sacrament. It is a martyrdom for me to think that He is so little loved, that so many hearts reject His pure love and are unmindful or scornful of Him. At least, if I loved Him, my heart would be consoled in its suffering, but I am the most ungrateful and unfaithful of all creatures, for I live a most sensual life of self-love. I feel constantly urged to suffer, and yet the terrible revulsions of my lower nature make my crosses so heavy and painful that I would succumb a thousand times if the adorable heart of my Jesus did not strengthen me and help me in all my needs. And my heart is always athirst for suffering, even amid my continual sufferings; and my soul suffers great anguish not to be able yet to be severed from its body. I can make no more rigorous sacrifice than the sacrifice of my life, and yet I accept [to live] until the day of judgment, if my God so wills, although the thought of separation from my Sovereign Good is harder for me than a thousand deaths."

In another letter to Mother de Saumaise, dated August 10, 1684, and addressed to Dijon, she speaks of the cross, her favorite subject:

"O my dear Mother, if its true value were known, everyone would not flee from it and reject it so freely; but on the contrary, it would be so greatly cherished and loved that everyone could find happiness only in the cross, and rest only on the cross, and would have no other wish than to die in His arms, scorned and abandoned by all."

We could continue making many more similar citations. Margaret Mary's whole soul shines through them. She was a reparative soul, a soul united to the cross. And to use the words of St. John of the Cross once more: she was truly "the beloved transformed into her Beloved."

FOR THE SOULS IN PURGATORY

At this point we should point out that Margaret Mary had a great and tender devotion to the souls in purgatory throughout her life. Her letters refer to them over and over. If we are to believe her—and we should not hesitate to do so—she was in direct contact with the souls in purgatory for whom she was praying. The following letter, among others, corroborates this. It was addressed to Mother de Saumaise and dated May 2, 1683:

"My soul is filled with such great joy that I find it hard to contain it within me. Allow me, good Mother, to share this joy with your heart, which is one with mine in the heart of our Lord. This morning, Good Shepherd Sunday, two of my good suffering friends came to say farewell as I was waking up, because on this day the supreme Shepherd was to welcome them into His eternal sheepfold together with over a million others, in whose company they were singing hymns of inexpressible delight. One of them was good Mother Philiberte Emmanuel de Monthoux, the other, my sister, Jane Catherine Gâcon, who kept repeating these words: *'Love triumphs, love possesses, love in God rejoices.'* The other said: *'Blessed are the dead who die in the Lord and the nuns who live and die in exact observance of their rules.'* They want me to tell you for them: *'Death can separate friends, but it cannot disunite them.'* This is from the good Mother to you. And my sister Jane Catherine: *'I will still be a good daughter to you in heaven, as you have been a good mother to me on earth.'*

"If you knew how much my soul was enraptured with joy, for as I talked with them I saw them gradually being drowned and engulfed in glory, like someone drowning in a vast ocean. They ask you to say, in thanksgiving to the most august Trinity, one Te Deum, one Laudate and three Gloria Patri. And as I begged them to remember us, they said to me, as their last message: that *ingratitude has never entered heaven!*"

These last words are precisely why the Catholic Church has embraced devotion to the saints.

It is not unimportant to note that Sister Jane Catherine of the monastery at Paray had died on January 18th of that year, while Mother de Monthoux, the superior at the monastery of Annecy, had died on February 5th. As the letter was dated May 2, 1683, we can calculate the time the two nuns spent in purgatory. It seems their punishments were not all of the same severity. At least this can be surmised from the conclusion of Margaret Mary's letter: "But if you knew the pain of this other one whom you know...it is beyond expression. Alas! Give me a few drops of water to refresh her, because I am burning with her and I cannot help her!"[1]

On November 4, 1683, probably in answer to a request from Mother de Saumaise on the fate of

1. We do not know to whom she is referring, but it must surely have been a nun.

Mother Boulier, who had died on September 7th, Margaret Mary answered:

"I think I should rejoice with you over your good fortune in having such a powerful advocate in heaven in the person of your late greatly honored Mother Anne Seraphine Boulier, rather than share in the sorrow caused you by separation from such a holy friend."

THE FIRST IMAGE OF THE SACRED HEART

As this admirable correspondence continues, we learn that Margaret Mary was convinced that Mother de Saumaise had been chosen by God to perpetuate the work of Father La Colombière. For the good mother knew Margaret Mary so well that she had completely adopted her views on devotion to the Sacred Heart. In fact, she was spreading it in her monastery at Dijon. It was she who initiated official petitions at Rome to obtain a liturgical feast in honor of the Sacred Heart. In March, 1687, Margaret Mary wrote to her as follows:

"All my prayers and everything I can do seem to be directed toward this goal alone, to establish the reign of the Sacred Heart; and now to obtain the approbation of the request you have made to Rome on this matter. I am not failing to ask the most sacred Virgin and our blessed Father La Colombière to take an interest in it, and I hope he will be of very great help to us. For, just as you are taking his place on earth, I think he also is taking yours in heaven to love and glorify this divine heart."

A little while later, Margaret Mary acclaimed with joy the publication of a booklet by Sister Jane Magdalene Joly, prepared under the direction of Mother de Saumaise at Dijon. This little book contained litanies in honor of the Sacred Heart and other prayers. Mother de Soudeilles, another of Margaret Mary's regular correspondents, had the same prayers printed at Moulins in honor of the Sacred Heart. So devotion to the Sacred Heart was first practiced at the Visitation monasteries of Dijon, Moulins, and Semur-en-Auxois where Mother Greyfié was superior, as well, of course, as at Paray-le-Monial. It was at Dijon that images of the Sacred Heart were first made.

When Margaret Mary received these images, she was delighted. On January 17, 1688, she wrote the following to Mother de Saumaise:

"I cannot express the sweet rapture of joy I felt at the sight of these holy images, which inspired me to bless you a thousand times in my soul, which deems yours so fortunate in this success, for it is yours alone together with all the graces it will draw down on your dear soul. And for that good sister—Sister Jane Magdalene Joly—I think, if I am not mistaken, that she has given Him more pleasure by what she has done in His honor than she had yet been able to do by all the actions of her life. And I think the Sacred Heart will make her an eternal monument to His mercies, for it seems to me He loves her tenderly and in return wants her to love Him alone and constantly. Ah! my dear Mother, what delight it is to this divine heart who will reward these delights with eternal and incomprehensible treasures."

ROME'S ANSWER

We have seen that the monastery of Dijon had addressed a petition directly to Rome, asking nothing less than the institution of a feast and devotion in honor of the Sacred Heart throughout the universal Church. Obviously, this was rushing matters somewhat, and Rome was not accustomed to such haste.

The Holy See answered that first this devotion had to be established publicly in the diocese, with the Bishop's permission. At that time, the Ordinary of Dijon was the Bishop of Langres. It was further stated that when this devotion had been successfully practiced there for a while, it would be possible to obtain the permissions necessary for its confirmation. This was an approbation in principle, at least. Rome had no objection to the request itself, as it had been presented. However, the fervent adorers of the Sacred Heart were a little disappointed. But Margaret Mary, her hopes unshaken, comforted Mother de Saumaise in a letter dated in August, 1688:

"Indeed, my good Mother, is your kind heart greatly disappointed by Rome's refusal concerning our adorable Savior? It seems to me, if I am not mistaken, that He wants me to console you on His behalf by telling you what has also consoled me. After receiving this news, which was a sword that pierced my heart with great pain, I went and prostrated myself before His image to tell Him my complaints.

"But I received this answer: 'Why are you distressed about what will be to my greater glory? Now, there is an effort to honor and love me with no other support than love itself, and this pleases me very much; but this fervor could grow cold...and this would deeply wound my divine heart, which is a burning furnace of pure love and could not endure it.... I shall rekindle this fire in all hearts, by all these privileges and even greater ones; and I shall not fail to reward the efforts made to this end. So remain at peace!' This is what I thought I heard said, and I remained uncertain whether I would have the consolation of seeing [this peace]. But the important thing is that He be satisfied. Then, I too shall delight in His contentment even though I am deprived of others."

DEVOTION TO THE SACRED HEART SPREADS

Margaret Mary was not to see her hopes fulfilled during her lifetime. But her expectations were ultimately realized and her obedience to the wishes of heaven was rewarded.

The feast of the Sacred Heart had already been established in the diocese of Langres, and hence at Dijon, within its jurisdiction. In 1693, three years after Margaret Mary's death, a papal brief addressed to the monastery at Dijon enriched this feast with precious indulgences, and extended the privilege to all Visitation monasteries. As a result of this favor granted by Pope Innocent XII, the feast was established in most of these convents. Confraternities were soon formed in many places, which received new approbations from the Holy See. Then cities, dioceses, and entire nations began to clamor for the institution of the feast of the Sacred Heart.

In 1765 Pope Clement XIII introduced the feast at Rome. Finally, in 1856, Pope Pius IX extended the feast to the entire Church. So devotion to the Sacred Heart became a permanent part of Catholic liturgy and devotion.

There are many charming incidents we could cite in the history of the growth of this devotion. In view of our intention to discuss only events that occurred during Margaret Mary's lifetime, we shall merely cite a few interesting facts.

On August 21, 1689, Margaret Mary wrote to Sister F.M. de la Barge at Moulins:

"I must share with you a fact to His glory that will give you an occasion for blessing Him. It is that I gave one of the Dijon books to a lady from Lyons. She in turn showed it to a young Father,[1] who showed it to his schoolboys in Lyons. They liked it so much that they made many copies of it, both the litanies and the prayers, which they recited with great devotion. And these children showed them to others whose devotion grew so strong that, since they couldn't make enough copies to meet the need, they turned to the lady who had this book, asking to know about devotion to the Sacred Heart of our Lord Jesus Christ, because they wanted to

1. This was probably the Jesuit Father Croiset.

have some of these books printed, even gladly offering to pay the expense.

"And a young artisan devoted himself to it with so much enthusiasm that there was no gainsaying his devotion. And having addressed himself to one of the most famous publishers of Lyons about this project, the latter was so moved with love for this divine heart that he took it upon himself to cover the expense, and this led to a pious battle between the young man who had undertaken to do it and himself. But having finally won his point, he asked for a copy of this book on the Sacred Heart and went to see one of his friends, to make some additions to it. And he pressed his friend so hard that he could not refuse, and it is a very holy religious who has written this addition. And some of them have been recently printed, and they are very beautiful and well bound, and the sales were so great that since they were printed the second time, there were none left by June 19th, and they are going to be printed a third time...."

This letter certainly rings like a cry of victory. And it gives a vivid idea of the ordinary procedure by which devotion to the Sacred Heart has been disseminated. The young Jesuits were the most enthusiastic propagandists. The children in the schools responded eagerly to their teaching. Devotion to the Sacred Heart was offering precious nourishment to the piety of the faithful and proving useful in the training of youth. Books about the devotion were read avidly. The litanies and prayers in honor of the loving heart of Christ were widely recited.

Another of Margaret Mary's letters confirms this. It was written on October 22, 1689, to Mother M. F. Dubuysson, superior of the Visitation at Moulins:

"Finally, my dear Mother, it is consoling to hear the successful progress of this beautiful devotion. We are informed from Lyons that it is like a miracle to see how everyone is embracing it with fervor and eagerness. Three or four cities have been mentioned to us where these books are going to be printed, including Marseilles. And a thousand have been taken for that one place. And of twenty-seven religious houses in that city, there is not one that has not accepted this devotion, and they have been so eager that some of them have erected altars, others are dedicating chapels to it; and as soon as the people of Marseilles heard about it, they urged their preachers to give them exhortations to thoroughly explain this devotion to them, which, in less than two weeks, spread so rapidly that an unbelievable number of devout persons receive Holy Communion every first Friday. And it has been said that it is going to be established in all the houses of the reverend Jesuit Fathers, who even have the young fathers who do not say Mass receive Communion every first Friday.

"I have wanted to tell you a few words about all these fortunate developments so that you may bless our sovereign Master for them, to whom I beg you to ask that He take my life rather than let me always be an obstacle to Him, as indeed I am to His great plans by my infidelities, ingratitudes, and resistances, which make up the entire fabric of my life...."

It was necessary to cite this last letter to show Margaret Mary's continual desire to humiliate herself before her divine Master, so as to leave to Him alone all the glory of this growing devotion to His heart.

But her Jesus sent her the most touching rewards. For example, He inspired priests in distant places and completely unknown to her to write her that they were offering the holy Sacrifice every month for her intentions. Knowing her, we can be sure that nothing could have touched her more deeply, confirming her faith and love. On February 23, 1689, she wrote to her beloved Mother de Saumaise:

"I admit to you in confidence that if His merciful kindness did not send me the charitable help of holy souls who pray for me, I could not subsist. He is so kind that He does not let me lack anything, having inspired holy religious to offer the holy Sacrifice of the Mass for my intentions every Friday, and without my knowing about it, so that I shall have four Masses a month during my life, unless they die before me. There are some that I have never seen. They have written to me that they never received so many graces as they have since practicing this charity."

This brings us to the very important question of "the Promises of the Sacred Heart." Margaret Mary had foretold that devotion to the Sacred Heart would produce much fruit in those who practiced it. She had been taken at her word, and already the promises she had made in the name of the Sacred Heart were being abundantly fulfilled.

We shall now devote a special chapter, one of the most important in this small book, to a study of these promises.

7

The Promises of the Sacred Heart

A FEW NECESSARY REMARKS

Before discussing the Promises of the Sacred Heart in his work entitled *La Spiritualité chrétienne,* Reverend P. Pourrat asks what value they may have. He then states his opinion in the following passage:

"To answer this question, we must distinguish, among the private revelations made to the saints, those that have been approved in some manner by the Church, and those that have received no approbation from the Church.

"The former must be considered authentic. In approving them, the Church guarantees their divine character and veracity. Included among them are the three great apparitions of the Sacred Heart to the saint of Paray, reported above.[1] The Church has indirectly guaranteed their reality by approving devotion to the Sacred Heart, by instituting the Feast of the Heart of Jesus, and by authorizing the devotion of the first Fridays of the month and the practice of the Holy Hour. As we know, all of these

1. Father Pourrat enumerates only three great apparitions, for he does not mention the second, which is among those recorded in the present book. He does point out that a number of authors have acknowledged four, and we agree with them.

practices were requested in these three apparitions of our Lord to St. Margaret Mary.

"But the Church has never made a positive pronouncement as to the value of the 'Promises of the Sacred Heart.' As we shall see, these promises are certainly included in the authentic writings of the saint. They are therefore eminently deserving of our respect. However, they remain private revelations, whose veracity is not absolutely certain. It is therefore quite permissible for the faithful to put their trust in these promises, to nourish their devotion on them, without believing in them as they believe the Gospel."[1]

For our part, as will be seen, we would be inclined to make distinctions among Margaret Mary's various affirmations.

OVERALL VIEW

In order to get an overall view of the promises of the Sacred Heart, we must read the following letter, probably written in 1689, and addressed by Margaret Mary to her spiritual director, who was then Father Rolin of the Society of Jesus, the same who had commanded her to write her autobiography.

"My Reverend Father, I wish I could tell everything I know about this beautiful devotion to the Sacred Heart of Jesus, and reveal to the whole world the treasures of grace that Jesus Christ holds in this adorable heart, and that He wants to pour forth profusely to all who will practice it!

"I beseech you, my Reverend Father, do not fail to do everything to inspire everyone to practice it.

"Jesus Christ made known to me in a manner that is not open to doubt that it was chiefly through the Fathers of the Society of Jesus that He wanted to establish this solid devotion everywhere, and

1. P. Pourrat, *La Spiritualité chrétienne*, Vol. IV, pp. 413-414.

through it to acquire an infinite number of faithful servants, of perfect friends, and perfectly grateful children.

"The treasures of blessings and graces the Sacred Heart contains are infinite. I do not know any practice of devotion in the spiritual life that is better suited to raise a soul to the highest perfection in a short time, and enable it to experience the true delights to be found in the service of Jesus Christ.

"Yes, I say with assurance, if it were known how pleasing this devotion is to Jesus Christ, there is not one Christian who has any love at all for this lovable Savior who would not hasten to practice it. Above all, see to it that persons in the religious life embrace it, for they will derive so much help from it that no other means will be needed to restore primitive fervor and exact observance in even the most unruly communities, and to lift to the heights of perfection those communities that live in the most exact observance of their rule.

"My divine Savior has given me to understand that those who labor for the salvation of souls will have the gift of touching even the most hardened hearts and will have wonderful success in their work if they themselves are filled with a tender devotion to His divine heart.

"As for lay persons, they will find by means of this beautiful devotion all the help they need for their state of life, peace in their families, consolation in their labors, the blessings of heaven on all their undertakings, consolation in their troubles. And it is in this Sacred Heart that they will find their refuge throughout their life and especially at the hour of death. Ah! How sweet it is to die after a lifetime of constant devotion to the heart of the One who is to judge us! Finally, it is evident that anyone who has for Jesus Christ a grateful love such as is shown for Him by devotion to the Sacred Heart will certainly receive all sorts of help from heaven."

This letter, some of whose details are confirmed in other letters written by the saint, contains all the essentials of the *"Promises of the Sacred Heart."* The historians and commentators who have studied them usually present the following categories of promises:

Father Pourrat says: "They concern priests, families, religious communities, and the Catholic faithful in general."[1]

Archbishop Gauthey, an eminent expert in all matters relating to Margaret Mary, enumerates these promises as follows:

"There are promises for those who are laboring to save souls. There are some for religious communities. There are some addressed to the faithful in general. Finally, still others concern the coming of His kingdom in the world."[2]

But the fulfillment of these magnificent promises depends on certain conditions: "To benefit from these promises," Father Pourrat explains, "one must have authentic devotion to the divine heart."[3]

But what are we to understand—indeed, what did the holy messenger of the Sacred Heart understand—by this "authentic devotion"? Here is the key to all the revelations. If we reflect on it, we shall readily see that these promises are in harmony with all that is deepest in our Christian faith. First, devotion to the Sacred Heart is nothing else than devotion to the Love of Christ. It can flourish only as a grateful love for Christ. The Promises of the Sacred Heart are a return for love.

It is not surprising, therefore, that spiritual *perfection,* that is, holiness, is promised to all who practice this devotion. For perfect holiness can and does exist only in souls that love, and by virtue of this love.

1. *Loc. cit.,* p. 414.

2. Archbishop Gauthey, *Le Sacré-Coeur de Jesus,* Paris, Téqui, 1916, p. 414.

3. P. Pourrat, *La Spiritualité chrétienne,* Vol. IV, p. 414.

Let us allow Margaret Mary to explain this to us once more, before considering the promises in detail. How does she visualize "true devotion" to the Sacred Heart?

PURE LOVE

In a letter probably written in March, 1689, a year before Margaret Mary's death, we have such an explanation. The letter, addressed to Sister de la Barge at Moulins, clearly shows that devotion to the Sacred Heart is no mere sentimental outpouring of love for the heart of Jesus. On the contrary, it involves total identification with Him. There is no true devotion to the Sacred Heart without "pure love," without a continually more perfect union with the "supreme Good."

Let us read attentively:

"May love, glory and praise be rendered forever to the heart that is love, all loving, and worthy of all love, of our adorable Savior, for the good it will effect in souls by establishing the reign of His pure love in hearts of good will....

"But forgive me, dear friend, for all I can say to you is that total death to self will raise you to union with your supreme Good. In forgetting yourself, you will possess Him, and in abandoning yourself to Him He will possess you."[2]

If we think about it, it is easy to see that the Promises of the Sacred Heart are simply expressions of divine truth. Margaret Mary tells us that through this devotion we are sure to advance toward perfection, to ascend toward holiness. We believe this. Inasmuch as it is a devotion of pure love, it is the way to holiness.

Let us clearly understand: Margaret Mary's promises, made in the name of the Sacred Heart, are not some sort of bait offered to our yearnings for *exterior* graces and blessings. These may or may not follow, depending on what is best for us. But this is not what the saint is telling us in her divine Master's name. She is really repeating what Christ Himself has said in the profound words that are so rarely understood: "Whoever loses his life for my sake...will preserve it" (Mark 8:35). To lose one's life for Jesus Christ is to love Him for Himself, it is to love Him with a "pure love."

There is no use imagining that "true devotion to the Sacred Heart" can be anything else but this. And once we admit this truth the promises of the Sacred Heart, as the historians have enumerated them, are no longer mere "private revelations," as was said earlier. They are identical with Christ's promises recorded in His Gospel.

Let us now see how Margaret Mary explains to Sister de la Barge how she understands the practice of this devotion:

"Go therefore with great faith and loving trust to surrender yourself to the mercy of His providence, to be a field He can cultivate as He pleases, and without any resistance on your part, clinging humbly and peacefully to His good pleasure, hidden in the sacred darkness of your love for your abjection. For I cannot but believe ever more strongly that that is where He wants you and where He looks at you with satisfaction, especially when these precious humiliations fill your poor heart with bitterness."

So this is what she understood by the "blessings" this devotion would obtain for all who practice it! These "precious humiliations," this love of abjection—so difficult to anyone who does not have pure love, or rather impossible to conceive without it—this "bitterness" in the heart accepted for love of Christ: all this brings us to the very center of true devotion to the Sacred Heart.

"But be of good courage, the medicines most helpful to health are often most bitter to the taste. Finally, God wants so much to possess your heart that He will make it find only bitterness in creatures and in all things of earth so that, drawing away all your heart's affections, it will remain completely lost in Him, in loving union with His abjection. And the bitterness you are experiencing rejoices me because it is giving you the means of winning a greater victory."

HOW THIS DEVOTION IS TO BE PRACTICED

Continuing her letter to Sister de la Barge, Margaret Mary came to the practices she recommended to her in the name of our Lord, so that she might really understand this devotion to His Sacred Heart.

"In response to your desire to be given some practices, I have spent some time in our chapel of the Sacred Heart for you. But my sins make me unworthy to hear His voice, and the only thought that came to me was that He cherishes your dear soul and will be pleased if every day during this season of Lent you make three visits to Him, either before His image, or before the Most Blessed Sacrament.

"The first visit [will be] to ask Him that this divine heart may be a channel through which the eternal Father continually pours out His mercies on the hardened hearts of sinners, to bring them to a love and knowledge of Him.

"The second visit will be to pray for the establishment of His reign of charity and love in our institute.

"And the third [will be] to offer yourself to Him as a victim of holocaust to be consumed on the cross of your abjection by the fire of His pure love. And you can do all this in spirit."

We should note that in recommending these devotional practices, Margaret Mary does not tell her friend to ask anything for herself except to become a "victim of holocaust." The overriding thought is the desire for the conversion of sinners, and the coming of the kingdom of Christ.

There is a complete disregard for self in this devotion. And we shall not be distorting the saint's deepest intentions if we say that without this total self-forgetfulness there is no pure love, and consequently no true devotion to the divine heart.

Seen in this light, the Promises of the Sacred Heart are free of any extraneous elements. They are absolute truths. The fruits of this devotion to the Sacred Heart are not a kind of bonus or reward coming from the outside. There is not and cannot be any self-interested calculation in the practice of this devotion, if it is to be correctly understood.

No one can say to God: "Lord, You see that I have great devotion to Your Sacred Heart, so You must fulfill Your promises. Do for me what You have announced through Your servant Margaret Mary. Grant me such and such a favor." Such a bargain is clearly contrary to the devotion to the Sacred Heart as understood by Margaret Mary and explained in her letters. The Promises of the Sacred Heart are always fulfilled, we boldly claim, even though they were made known in private revelations to our saint. For these private revelations, as we have tried to demonstrate, differ in no way from the official and incontestable revelations of the Gospels.

We shall show this in detail when we turn to the specific promises addressed by the Sacred Heart to various categories of persons.

FOR PRIESTS

In the first place, there are the promises addressed to priests. Margaret Mary has said:

"My divine Master has revealed to me that those who are working for the salvation of souls will labor with success and will have the art of touching even the most hardened hearts, if these priests have a tender devotion to His Sacred Heart, and if they work to inspire and establish it everywhere."

Let us translate this into the terms we have already defined. Priests who have a tender devotion to the Sacred Heart are priests who are consumed with love for our Lord, who surrender themselves totally to Him, who do what Margaret Mary recommended to her nun-friend at Moulins—three visits a day: the first, to ask the divine heart to be "the channel through which the eternal Father continually pours out His mercies on the hardened hearts of sinners, to draw them to a love and knowledge of Him"; the second, to beg Him "to establish His reign of charity and love" in the milieu they are evangelizing; and the third, to offer themselves to Him as "victims of holocaust."

In other words, Margaret Mary is saying that priests must be saints—and they can be or become saints through "a tender devotion to the Sacred Heart" if they understand this devotion as we have explained it, and thus discover the art of "touching even the hardest hearts."

The only great suffering anyone who loves the Sacred Heart can have is not to be a saint! Love has an irresistible power of contagion, and the powerhouse of pure love is none other than the heart of Jesus.

Margaret Mary was so convinced of this that she spoke of it repeatedly, as it concerned priests.

In a letter to Father Croiset, the young Jesuit who was to write her first biography in 1691, she said:

"Since you want me to tell you what I think of your plans to honor this divine heart, if I am not mistaken, they are so pleasing that I hope this will be one of the means He [Jesus] wants to use in this devotion. He wants to snatch a great many souls from perdition, undermining Satan's dominion, so as to lead them by His sanctifying graces back to the path of eternal salvation. This is what He seems to have promised to His unworthy slave, showing this devotion to her as one of the ultimate efforts of His love toward men: by showing them His divine heart pierced with love for their salvation, He wants to assure their salvation. He wills to let nothing perish that has been consecrated to His divine heart. He will distribute sanctifying and salutary graces to men in abundance, be their safe refuge at the hour of death, and welcome them and defend them from their enemies. But to attain this, one must live in conformity to His holy maxims."

This means that devotion to the Sacred Heart is meaningless unless one lives according to the "sacred maxims" of the Gospel and unless one obeys Christ's command: "If a man wishes to come after me, he must take up his cross, and follow in my steps" (Mark 8:34). There is no true devotion to the Sacred Heart without renunciation, without the spirit of penance, without the consuming love exhibited by so many of the saints. We might simply cite as examples St. Louis Mary Grignion de Montfort, the great converter of early 17th-century France, St. Leonard of Port Maurice, and St. John Mary Vianney. As for the last-named, the Curé of Ars, he was looked down on as a rather stupid country pastor. But all his great victories over unbelief, over "hardened hearts," must be attributed to his holiness, to his powerful love, in a word, to his devotion to the Sacred Heart.

Margaret Mary was very explicit in her writings, and even more in her actions. She made it clear that the friends of the Sacred Heart are friends of the cross, and they must love to suffer with their divine Master.

Writing in this vein to Mother Greyfié, who had once been her superior at Paray, she said:

"It seems to me that [the Sacred Heart] made me see that several names were inscribed within it because of their zeal to bring it honor, and that for this reason, [Jesus] would never permit these names to be erased. But He did not tell me that His friends would have nothing to suffer, for He wants them to find their greatest happiness in sharing His own bitter sufferings."

Now, the purpose of devotion to the Sacred Heart on the part of priests can never be simply to find a short cut to a successful apostolate. This would be a total distortion of Margaret Mary's thought, as well as that of Christ who revealed it to His faithful servant. Indeed, it would be to diminish and parody its intent. There can be no devotion to the Sacred Heart without a love of the cross. And it is through love of the cross that this devotion was to attain all the successes promised to those who would practice it.

It is quite true, therefore, that the "Promises of the Sacred Heart" presented to the world through St. Margaret Mary are identical with the promises of the Gospels.

AN AUTHORITATIVE COMMENTARY

It was in this sense that Archbishop Gauthey commented on the first promise in his allocutions on the Sacred Heart during World War I. He said:

"When all priests and religious have really understood this promise, when they have become so completely penetrated by it, to the point that every act of their ministry is inspired with a tender—that is the divine word—a tender devotion to the Sacred Heart of Jesus, the Catholic world will be renewed in the fervor of the most beautiful Christian eras."

And as he was speaking in time of war, he added:

"When our priests take off their uniforms to return to their cassocks, these cassocks shot through with bullet holes will clothe hearts burning with love for the heart of Jesus, men who will be apostles of this Sacred Heart and become powerful converters of souls, for the religious and moral regeneration of France."

Have priests lived up to this hope? It is hard to say. The spiritual transformation of a people takes place slowly and invisibly. There are no sudden changes in the psyche of a nation. And yet a threefold renewal is apparent in the Church. There is, of course, the liturgical renewal which is obvious to everyone, a Biblical renewal that is unmistakable, and finally a mystical renewal. This mystic renewal has found expression in a growing interest in mystical studies, such as the present biography, and above all in the life of Jesus,[1] the life of the Blessed Virgin Mary, and such great mystics as St. Teresa of Avila and St. John of the Cross.

The ferment of spiritual renewal is working, and no one can foresee where it will lead. Devotion to the Sacred Heart, understood in the specific sense set forth above, is certainly the wellspring of all the good that is being accomplished in the world at this time. God continues to ask for *reparative souls,* souls united to the Savior's redemptive cross.

PROMISES FOR RELIGIOUS COMMUNITIES

While there are many reparative souls living in the world, there is greater reason to look for them in cloisters and religious communities. For religious communities have a specific function to perform within the Church. We might say that whereas the hierarchy and the clergy form the brain of the Mystical Body of Christ, religious communities are its heart, whose capacity to love is always alive and fully active. A community that loses some of its fervor and slackens its observance of its rule imperils that portion of the warmth of the Church's soul that resides within it.

Now, the Sacred Heart made specific promises to religious communities. This is certainly proof of the importance Christ attaches to the religious life.

1. The great success of a book like Daniel-Rops' *Jesus and His Times* is an indication of the growing interest in the divine story of Christ's life.

What did He say to religious through Margaret Mary? In a letter to Father Croiset, she has said:

"He promises that He will pour the sweet balm of charity upon all religious communities that honor Him and place themselves under His special protection; that He will keep their hearts united, making them all one with His heart, and will deflect the bolts of divine justice from them, restoring them to grace when they have fallen from it."

Here we find the basic aspects of devotion to the Sacred Heart.

Writing to Mother Greyfié at Semur, sometime during the year 1685, Margaret Mary said:

"He made me understand that His Sacred Heart is the Saint of saints, the *Saint of Love!* that He wanted to be known now as the *Mediator* between God and men, for He is all powerful to make their peace, by averting the punishments that our sins have called down on us, and obtaining mercy for us."

Religious communities must focus their attention above all on these words: *the Saint of saints, the Saint of love, the Mediator.* Now, Christ is all of these by Himself alone and through His own power. But He deigns to let us share in His mysterious action within the created world. Together with Him, religious communities are part of the *Saint of saints*, that is, of the most intimate center of adoration and love addressed to the Most Blessed Trinity. They are part of the *Saint of love*, and are one with Him. With Him, they perform a service of mediation on behalf of the sinners of the whole world.

Actually, most of the religious communities of France are consecrated to the Sacred Heart. It is eminently desirable that every person consecrated to God, in monasteries and convents of men and women, be able to say what Margaret Mary said in the above-quoted letter to Mother Greyfié:

"If you only knew, my good Mother, how powerfully I am impelled to love the Sacred Heart of our

Lord Jesus Christ! It seems to me that life is given to me only for this purpose...."

PROMISES FOR FAMILIES

While the Sacred Heart has special favors for His priests and for those consecrated to God in the religious life, He does not forget the great multitude of the Christian faithful. After all, it is for them, for their good, for the forgiveness of their sins, for their eternal salvation, that priests and members of religious communities receive special graces. A man is not a priest for his own sake; one does not enter the religious life for purely personal reasons. The Church forms a single whole. In Margaret Mary's writings there is a continual vision of souls to be won for Jesus; that is, for their own best interests, for the attainment of their deepest aspirations.

What does the Sacred Heart say to the faithful through Margaret Mary?

"By means of this beautiful devotion they will obtain all the helps they need for their state of life, that is: peace in their families, solace in their labors, the blessings of heaven on all their undertakings, consolation in their troubles. And it is precisely in this Sacred Heart that they will find their refuge during life and above all at the hour of death."

If all the faithful knew these wonderful promises, they would certainly make every effort to obtain their fulfillment. Peace in the family, in the first place. Our saint was very positive on this point: "He will reunite divided families and protect and help those who might be in some need and who turn to Him trustingly."

Here again, let us emphasize we are not talking about some "recipe" for earthly success. Nothing could be further from the essential truth of this devotion of love. Catholics, both individuals and families, who want to practice this devotion must be guided by the principles we have already set forth. It is all summed up in the great law of love. The Sacred Heart is the source of love that God has placed at our service and within our reach. It is in this heart that we must—that all Christians without exception must—seek this twofold love. For Christ has said that whoever practices this love fulfills "the Law and the prophets," in other words, the entire will of the Creator for them. Of course, we are speaking of the command to love God with all our strength, and our neighbor as ourselves.

PROMISES OF A MORE LIMITED SORT

The promises we have so far enumerated are obviously in close harmony with the promises of the Gospels, and in our view they can be considered as absolute and certain of fulfillment. For example, priests who become saints through this devotion to the Sacred Heart will obtain abundant fruit in their ministries and will touch even the hardest hearts. The universal experience of history confirms it. It is not human talent that wins souls to Jesus Christ, but divine grace. And the most efficacious means by which grace penetrates into men's minds and hearts is through the holiness of those who preach and propagate it.

The same holds true for the promises addressed to religious communities and to all the Christian faithful in general. Religious communities that faithfully practice devotion to the Sacred Heart will certainly maintain their fervor, and families that revere the Sacred Heart will be preserved in peace. It is almost a tautology to affirm it. The great secret is to love. And devotion to the Sacred Heart is simply the secret of loving with Jesus Christ.

For these reasons, it hardly seems the promises so far mentioned can be called "*private revelations.*" They coincide with the most certain and most divine revelations.

Two of the promises made to Margaret Mary, however, are of a different sort, namely: the promise concerning Communion on first Fridays, and the one concerning images of the Sacred Heart. As we see it, only these two promises fit into the description given by Father Pourrat, on pages 133-134 above. These are not general promises, like the others, but special favors attached to particular practices.

COMMUNIONS ON THE NINE FIRST FRIDAYS

"One Friday, during Holy Communion, He spoke these words to His unworthy slave, if she is not mistaken:

"'I promise you, in the excessive mercy of my heart, that my all-powerful love will grant to all who receive Holy Communion on the first Friday of the month for nine consecutive months, the grace of final penitence; they shall not die in disgrace and without receiving the sacraments. My divine heart shall be their safe refuge in their last moment.'"

Such a promise lies outside the scope of the great Gospel certitudes. Father Pourrat is unquestionably right in saying: "The Church has never made any declaration on the subject of this extraordinary promise which is valid, therefore, only as a private revelation. One should not, therefore, believe it as one believes an article of the Creed. The novena of Communions for nine months is certainly excellent. But when it is recommended, care should be taken to avoid any intimation that it will infallibly obtain by itself alone all the favors it specifies."[1]

Archbishop Gauthey makes similar reservations, which should be taken seriously:

"Here is a guarantee of salvation that all the faithful can accept. Undoubtedly, it demands a certain perseverance, and it will require effort, sometimes even hardship. But truly the prize is worth

1. P. Pourrat, *La Spiritualité chrétienne*, Vol. IV, p. 417.

the trouble. It is easy to understand what our Lord has in mind. He wants the faithful to receive Holy Communion more often, to be nourished with Himself, for that is how they will unite their own lives to His. There is good reason to believe that those who have been faithful to their intention of receiving Holy Communion for nine months in succession will afterwards be inclined to persevere in this practice."

Let us not attach an infallible efficacy to the formula: *Nine first Fridays in succession.* It would almost be a kind of superstition to stress this alone. And Margaret Mary had no intention of introducing what might be called a "vain observance." What Archbishop Gauthey sees above all is the efficacy of these Communions on nine first Fridays as developing the habit of frequent Communion and nurturing thereby an ever closer union with our Lord Jesus Christ.

At the same time, it cannot be denied that this devout practice of the nine first Fridays has been rewarded on many occasions by unexpected conversions and crowned by final perseverance in what seemed hopeless circumstances.

THE IMAGE OF THE SACRED HEART

Here again we shall cite Archbishop Gauthey, since he is one of the experts on the subject: "There is a special promise relating to the image of the Sacred Heart. Our Lord has declared to Blessed Margaret Mary that, '*wherever this image is exposed in order to be given special honor, it will draw down all sorts of blessings upon those who so honor it.*'"

Now, there is no question here of merely exhibiting the picture, as if it were some sort of "good luck charm." Margaret Mary has clearly said: "*in order to be given special honor.*" It is not the image in itself that matters. The reason "all sorts of blessings" will be poured out upon the house where this image is exposed is because of the honor given, because of the devotion rendered to the Sacred Heart.

Archbishop Gauthey goes on to say: "It is useless for us to claim to be intellectuals and scorn the role of the emotions in a spirit of proud condescension.... The image of the Sacred Heart is very expressive. It is a living picture, so to speak, well suited to inspire devotion, love, and gratitude toward God. And besides fulfilling an educational function, it is something more. By the merciful will of our Lord, it is a source of protection."

THE PROMISE TO LOUIS XIV AND TO FRANCE

Closely related to the promise made to all who would expose the image of the Sacred Heart in their homes, we should mention the special promise addressed to King Louis XIV and to France as a whole during Margaret Mary's own lifetime. As it happened, it is now only an historical incident whose expectations were never fulfilled. But since it is part of our saint's life, we cannot pass it over in silence.

The Friday after the Octave of Corpus Christi, during the year 1688, Margaret Mary wrote to Mother de Saumaise at Dijon, saying in part:

"He [our Lord] wants, it seems to me, to enter with pomp and magnificence into the house of princes and kings, to be honored there as much as He has been outraged, scorned, and humiliated during His passion, and to receive as much pleasure in seeing the great of the world abased and humiliated before Him, as the bitterness He felt when He saw Himself abased at their feet.

"'Make known to the eldest son of my heart'—[our Lord said]—speaking of our king—'that, just as his temporal birth was obtained through devotion to the merits of my holy childhood, likewise he will obtain his birth to grace and eternal glory by consecrating himself to my adorable heart, which wants to triumph over his, and to triumph as well over the hearts of the great of the earth through his intervention. [My heart] wants to reign in his palace, to be painted on his banners and engraved on his coat of arms, to make them victorious over all his enemies, knocking down these proud and arrogant heads, so he will triumph over all the enemies of the holy Church.'"

And Margaret Mary added:

"You will have reason to laugh, my good Mother, at my foolishness in telling you that, but I follow the inspiration that is given me to do so at this very instant."

We don't know whether Mother de Saumaise did feel like laughing when she read this message. But the *Life by the Contemporaries* does not mention this incident which has been referred to by many historians and preachers. In any event, our saint brought the matter up again in another letter to Mother de Saumaise in August, 1689. In this second letter, she said among other things:

"But since God chose the Reverend Father de la Chaise[1] to carry out this plan, by reason of the power He has given him over the heart of our great king, it will be up to him to bring it to success, by securing this glory for the divine heart of our Lord Jesus Christ.... It seems to me, my dear Mother, that you will be doing something very pleasing to this divine heart by using the means He has inspired you to use, of writing to my very honored Sister Superior of Chaillot àbout the plan that your charity points out to us. Besides, we must pray hard and have others pray for this intention."

So Mother de Saumaise, full of zeal for everything relating to devotion to the Sacred Heart, had

1. He was then the king's confessor.

adopted her confidante's idea. She had suggested turning to the superior at Chaillot for help, and even wrote to her. But nothing ever materialized. Perhaps the superior disregarded the suggestion, or perhaps Father de la Chaise, who knew his royal penitent very well, didn't think he could talk to him about it. Or maybe the king himself, engrossed with political and military affairs, simply paid no attention to it. In any event, nothing came of the proposal.

We have now covered all the *"Promises of the Sacred Heart"* made to Margaret Mary. From what we have said, we hope it is clear that these promises should be divided into two separate categories. The first group of promises, to which we have given most attention, really is a new presentation of the great Gospel promises. It is the law of love that finds expression in devotion to the Sacred Heart. It is the same law of love that gives to Christ's apostles the fruits they have a right to expect from their efforts. It is this same law that maintains religious communities in their pristine fervor, or restores them to it if they have become lukewarm. Finally, it is this love that sanctifies both families and individuals. On this point there can be no doubt or hesitation.

The same does not hold true for the promises which we have called "private." We refer to the promise of final perseverance attached to Communion on nine successive first Fridays, as well as the blessings of all sorts attributed to the exposition of the image of the Sacred Heart in homes.

Finally, we wonder if the promise made to the king of France, but whose conditions were never fulfilled, was really made to France as a nation, and perhaps in perpetuity? Certain men of judgment have thought it was.

There is one aspect of devotion to the Sacred Heart that remains to be mentioned. It is contained in the words Margaret Mary herself used to sum up our Lord's promises once and for all:

"This Sacred Heart will reign in spite of Satan and of all who will try to oppose it!"

This might be called the promise of promises, and it is really contained in Jesus Christ's own words to His apostles: "Take courage! I have overcome the world!" "The prince of this world has been condemned!" (Jn. 16:33, 11)

Epilogue

DEATH OF A SAINT

While Margaret Mary received many graces that were not meant for herself alone but for all of us, she was the first to benefit from them. Whatever she counseled others to do, she practiced herself to a supereminent degree. This applies to her recommendations to her sisters at the Visitation of Paray, or to the Ursulines, or to her brothers, one of whom became the mayor of Sainte-Marie-au-Bois, and the other the pastor of the church in the same village. And what she advised them all was this: Union with the Savior's cross, courageous acceptance of the trials of life in a spirit of penance and reparation. One of the articles of her own devotion to the Sacred Heart was the heroic vow of perfection, in which she emulated the great Teresa of Avila.

"I shall leave my superior complete liberty to dispose of me as seems best to her, humbly and indifferently accepting the tasks that obedience will give me, in spite of the frightful repugnance I feel for all these tasks."

She performed the functions of mistress of novices, and then returned to the infirmary, under the authority of the good but stern Sister Marest. Then, in 1687, she was named assistant for a second time.

And then what she dreaded more than anything else happened. She was being considered as the prospective superior of the monastery after Mother Melin's six-year term expired. On March 23, 1690, Margaret Mary saw our Lord presenting a cross to her. She accepted it, as always, without knowing what it was all about. But she learned soon afterward that this cross was to be her appointment as superior. She hastened to complain to our Lord about it, saying:

"Is it possible, O my God, that You should permit a creature like me to be in evidence as the head of a community? I beg of You to take this cross away from me; I am ready to accept any other."

Her prayer was answered. Another nun was elected by the community. But to her great disappointment, she was obliged to continue as assistant.

MARGARET MARY'S LAST LETTER

To help us understand her frame of mind and soul at this moment of her life, we shall quote a letter she wrote shortly before her death to her director, the Jesuit Father Rolin. It might well be called her "farewell to earth."

"I do not know what to think of the state in which I now find myself. Until now I have had three burning desires that were like three tyrants, making me suffer continual martyrdom and never giving me a moment's rest. These three desires were to love my God perfectly, to suffer greatly for love of Him, and to die of this burning love.

"But now, I find myself enjoying a tranquillity of heart that I cannot describe, and the cessation of all desires surprises me. I fear this supposed peace may be an effect of the insensitivity in which God sometimes leaves unfaithful souls; and I'm afraid that, through my great infidelities to His graces, I may have called this state down upon myself, which can be a kind of abandonment and reprobation. For I assure you that I can no longer will or desire anything in this world, although I clearly see that I lack everything as far as virtue is concerned. Sometimes I try to grieve over it, but I cannot, since it is not in my power, to so speak, to act. I feel only a perfect acquiescence to the good pleasure of God and an ineffable pleasure in suffering.

"The thought that consoles me from time to time is that the Sacred Heart of our Lord Jesus Christ will do everything for me, if I let Him have His way; He will love, desire, and will for me, and make up for all my failings."

A DEATH OF LOVE

We need only to read this letter to realize that here was a soul that had reached its full stature and had nothing more to expect from this earth; here was a soul ready for heaven. Everyone who loves can say that "his eternity has begun." As Bossuet used to say: "Let us love, let us love, and then we'll be doing during our earthly life what we shall be doing for all eternity." Margaret Mary had never ceased loving during her life. Toward the end, she was often heard to say: "I shall not live much longer, because I am not suffering at all any more."

On October 8, 1690, she had to take to her bed. But no one had any idea that she was near death. The doctor who was taking care of her declared after she died "that he had found no symptoms in her illness that threatened such an early end." He added "that he had no doubt that love of God was the sole cause of her death."

This *death of love* occurred on October 17, 1690, while she was receiving the last sacraments, at her own request. One of the last things she said summed up her blessed life and suggests the lesson we are to draw from it:

"I no longer need anything except God alone and to plunge into the heart of Jesus Christ!"

On Devotion to the Sacred Heart

HAURIETIS AQUAS

Encyclical Letter of His Holiness, Pius XII
by Divine Providence Pope
To the Venerable Brethren, the Patriarchs, Primates,
Archbishops, Bishops, and Other Local Ordinaries
in Peace and Communion with the Apostolic See

May 15, 1956

To our venerable brethren, the Patriarchs, Primates, Archbishops and other local Ordinaries in peace and communion with the Apostolic See: health and apostolic benediction.

"You shall draw waters with joy out of the Savior's fountains."[1] These words, in which the prophet Isaias in very expressive imagery foretold the manifold and rich gifts of God which the Christian era was to reap, spontaneously come to our mind as we recall the centenary of the proclamation in which our predecessor of immortal memory, Pius IX, gladly granting the petition of the Catholic world, ordered the celebration of the feast of the Sacred Heart throughout the whole Church.

AN INESTIMABLE GIFT

Those heavenly blessings which devotion to the Sacred Heart of Jesus pours into the souls of the faithful, purifying them, refreshing them with heavenly consolation and urging them to acquire all virtues, are too numerous to be counted. Mindful, therefore, of the wise words of the apostle St. James—"Every good gift and every perfect gift is from above, coming down from the Father of Lights"[2]—we rightly see in this devotion, which everywhere grows more fervent, the inestimable gift which the Incarnate Word, our divine Savior, as the sole Mediator of grace and truth between the heavenly Father and the human race, gave to the Church, His mystical bride, in recent times so that she could endure great trials and surmount difficulties. In virtue of this inestimable gift, the Church is able to manifest her ardent love for her divine Founder and in a fuller measure carry out the injunction given by Jesus Christ Himself, which St. John the Evangelist records: "Now on the last, the great day of the feast, Jesus stood and cried out, saying, 'If anyone thirst, let him come to me and let him drink who believes in me. As the Scripture says, *From within him there shall flow rivers of living water.*' He said this, however, of the Spirit whom they who believed in him were to receive."[3]

It was certainly not hard for those who heard Jesus speak these words, in which He promised that a fountain of "living water" would flow from within Him, to recall the words of the holy prophets Isaias, Ezechiel and Zachary foretelling the Messianic kingdom, and to recall also that rock from which water miraculously gushed forth when Moses struck it.[4]

A MOST EXCELLENT ACT OF RELIGION

Divine love has its origin in the Holy Spirit, who is the personified love of both the Father and the Son in the bosom of the august Trinity. Most aptly, then, does the Apostle of the Gentiles, echoing the words of Jesus Christ, attribute the infusion of charity in the souls of the faithful to this Spirit of love: "The charity of God is poured forth in our hearts by the Holy Spirit who has been given to us."[5]

This intimate bond which, according to Sacred Scripture, exists between the divine charity that must burn in the souls of the faithful and the Holy Spirit, who is love itself, clearly shows to all of us, venerable brothers, the real nature of the devotion which should be rendered to the Sacred Heart of Jesus Christ. For it is perfectly clear that this devotion, if we examine its proper nature, is a most excellent act of religion, inasmuch as it demands the full and absolute determination of surrendering and consecrating oneself to the love of the divine Redeemer whose wounded heart is the living sign and symbol of that love. It is likewise clear, even to a greater degree, that this devotion especially indicates that we must repay divine love with our own love.

Indeed, it flows from the very essence of love that the souls of men fully and completely submit to the rule of the Supreme Being, because the act of our love so depends upon the divine will that it forms, as it were, a certain oneness according to the words of Scripture, "He who cleaves to the Lord is one in spirit with him."[6]

I

The Church has always held devotion to the Sacred Heart of Jesus in such high regard and continues to esteem it so greatly that she strives to have this devotion flourish throughout the world, and to promote it in every way among Christian peoples. At the same time she is vigilant to safeguard it with all her strength against the charges of what is called *naturalism* and *sentimentalism*. In spite of this, it is nevertheless a deplorable fact that in the past and in our own time this most noble devotion has not been held in a place of honor and esteem among some Christians, and at times not even among those who claim to be animated by zeal for the Catholic religion and the acquiring of sanctity.

THE ERROR OF THOSE WHO CONTEND...

"If you knew the gift of God."[7] Venerable brothers, we, who by the hidden designs of God have been chosen as guardian and dispenser of that sacred treasure of faith and piety which the divine Redeemer entrusted to His Church, make these words our own. Through them, in keeping with the duty of our office, we admonish all those of our sons who are still led by preconceived opinions, and go so far at times as to consider devotion to the Sacred Heart of Jesus (which triumphing, as it were, over the errors and neglect of men has spread over His whole Mystical Body) as less suited—not to say detrimental—to the more pressing spiritual needs of the Church and the human race in our times.

...THAT THIS DEVOTION IS PURELY OPTIONAL

There are some who, because they join the very essence of this devotion to other forms of piety which the Church approves and encourages but does not command, put it on an equal footing with these other forms of piety and look upon it as some kind of additive which each one is free to use according to his own good pleasure.

...THAT IT IS USELESS OR IRRATIONAL

There are others, again, who assert that this devotion is burdensome and of little or no value, particularly for those who are serving as soldiers in the kingdom of God, motivated by the idea of working, to the utmost of their strength, resources and time, to defend, teach and spread Catholic doctrine, to inculcate Christian social teaching, and to promote those acts of religion and those undertakings which they consider much more necessary today. Then, too, there are those who, far from considering this devotion a powerful help for correctly forming and restoring Christian morals both in the private life of individuals and in the family circle, consider it rather as a form of piety springing from emotions and not from reasoned convictions and more suited, therefore, for women, because they see in it something unbecoming educated men.

...THAT IT IS TOO PASSIVE

There are still others also, who, since they consider that a devotion of this sort calls primarily for penance, expiation and other virtues which they call "passive" because they are not such as bear external fruits, conclude that it is unsuitable for nurturing the spiritual fervor demanded by our times, which ought to be directed toward visible and strenuous activity, the triumph of the Catholic Faith and the defense of Christian morals; indeed, as all know, these morals are readily tainted today by the fallacious attitudes of those who take an identical view of every form of religion (because the distinction of true and false in thought and action has been lost), and are pathetically contaminated by the principles of what are called atheistic *materialism* and *laicism.*

LEO XIII ANSWERS THESE OBJECTIONS

Venerable brothers, who does not see that such opinions are completely contrary to the teachings which our predecessors publicly proclaimed from this chair of truth when they approved the devotion to the Sacred Heart of Jesus? Who would dare call useless and less suitable to our time that piety which our predecessor of immortal memory, Leo XIII, declared "a most excellent form of religion" and in which he had no doubt there was to be found a powerful remedy to cure those very same evils which today, too—beyond doubt in an even greater and more violent manner—afflict and vex individuals and society? "This devotion," he said, "which we recommend to all, will be profitable for all."

He added these admonitions and exhortations which also apply to devotion to the Sacred Heart of Jesus: "Hence this force of evils, which has so long been weighing heavily upon us, demands that the help of One be sought by whose power it can be driven off. Who is He, but Jesus Christ, the only-begotten Son of God! 'For there is no other name under heaven given to men by which we must be saved' (Acts 4:12). We must then flee to Him, who is the Way, the Truth and the Life."[8]

THE MIND OF PIUS XI

Neither did our immediate predecessor of happy memory, Pius XI, declare this devotion less approved and suited to foster Christian piety. In an encyclical letter he wrote: "Is not the epitome of religion, and consequently the norm of the more perfect life, contained in that form of piety which more readily leads souls to acknowledge Christ the Lord and which more effectively inclines hearts to love Him more ardently and imitate Him more closely?"[9]

PROVIDENTIAL GROWTH OF THIS DEVOTION

This truth is as evident and clear to us as it was to our predecessors. When we became Pope and saw with pleasure that devotion to the Sacred Heart of Jesus had providentially increased among Christian peoples and was marching in triumph, so to speak, we were filled with joy at the graces which flowed to the Church from this devotion. We were pleased to note this in our very first encyclical.[10]

A NEW FERVOR

Through the years of our pontificate, filled not only with cares and anxieties but also with ineffable consolations, these blessings have not been diminished in number, power or splendor, but have rather been multiplied. Various movements have providentially started which are conducive to the adding of new fervor to this devotion and most aptly suited to the needs of our times. We mean organizations to promote culture, religion and charity, published articles which explain the historical, the ascetical or the mystical aspects which have bearing on this topic, and pious works of expiation.

We mention especially the proofs of deepest piety given by the Apostleship of Prayer, under whose auspices and care homes, colleges, institutions and at times whole nations were consecrated to the most Sacred Heart of Jesus. Not infrequently by letter, public addresses, and even by radio we have extended our paternal congratulations to these undertakings.[11]

11. St. Margaret Mary

"TO HIM BE GLORY"

Consequently, as we behold the rich abundance of salutary waters, that is, of heavenly gifts of divine love, flowing from the Sacred Heart of our Redeemer and permeating countless children of the Catholic Church (under the inspiration and operation of the Holy Spirit), we cannot refrain, venerable brothers, from exhorting you paternally to join us in giving glory and thanks to God, the giver of all good gifts. We join our sentiments with those of the Apostle of the Gentiles: "Now, to him who is able to accomplish all things in a measure far beyond what we ask or conceive, in keeping with the power that is at work in us—to him be glory in the Church and in Christ Jesus down through all the ages of time without end. Amen."[12]

SOLID FOUNDATIONS OF THE DEVOTION

But after we have duly thanked the eternal God, we wish through this encyclical to urge you, and all our dearly beloved children of the Church, to study diligently the teachings of Scripture, the Fathers and theologians—the solid foundations on which devotion to the Sacred Heart of Jesus rests.

For we are firmly convinced that only when we have thoroughly investigated the basic and profound nature of this devotion in the light of divinely revealed truth, only then, do we say, can we rightly and fully appreciate its incomparable excellence and its inexhaustible store of heavenly gifts. Only after piously meditating on the countless blessings flowing from this devotion can we worthily commemorate the first centenary of the celebration of the feast of the most Sacred Heart of Jesus throughout the universal Church.

A SALUTARY TEACHING

To give to the minds of the faithful a salutary teaching by virtue of which they can more easily and fully understand the true nature of this devotion and reap its abundant fruits, we shall explain those passages of the Old and New Testaments in which God's infinite love for mankind is revealed and set before us. We can, of course, never really study that love sufficiently. We shall then touch upon the chief points of the teaching of the Fathers and Doctors of the Church.

Finally, it will be our concern to show in its true light the close connection that exists between the kind of devotion to be shown to the heart of the divine Redeemer and the veneration due to His love and the love of the august Trinity for all men. For we think that only if the principal reasons for this noble form of piety and the foundations on which it rests are set forth in the light of Scripture and the teaching handed down in the Church can the faithful quite readily "draw waters with joy out of the Savior's fountains."[13]

To draw this water means to realize more fully the special importance which devotion to the Sacred Heart of Jesus has in the liturgy of the Church and in her internal and external life and activity, and so to be able to gather those spiritual fruits through which individuals can profitably renew their way of life, as the shepherds of the flock of Christ desire.

THE CHURCH ADORES...

That all may be able to understand more correctly the doctrine which the passages to be cited from the Old and New Testament proclaim in regard to this devotion, they must above all clearly understand the reason why the Church adores [*cultum latriae tribuit*] the heart of the divine Redeemer.

...THE SACRED HEART UNITED TO THE DIVINE PERSON

Now it is perfectly clear to you, venerable brothers, that the reason for this is twofold. The first reason, which also applies to the other sacred members of the body of Jesus Christ, rests on the teaching by which we know that His heart, as the noblest part of human nature, is hypostatically united to the Person of the divine Word and must therefore be adored in the same way in which the Church adores the Person of the Incarnate Son of God. We are dealing with an article of Catholic Faith, since this point was already solemnly defined in the general Council of Ephesus and the second Council of Constantinople.[14]

...THE SACRED HEART: SIGN AND SYMBOL OF LOVE

The second reason, which refers specifically to the heart of the divine Redeemer and in a special manner demands that adoration [*cultum latriae*] be given it, stems from the fact that His heart, more than all the other members of His body, is the natural sign and symbol of His boundless love for the human race. Our predecessor of immortal memory, Leo XIII, remarked: "In the Sacred Heart there is the symbol and the express image of the infinite love of Jesus Christ which moves us to love in return."[15]

GOD'S LOVE IMAGED IN SCRIPTURE

It is true that Scripture never makes express mention of a special devotion of veneration and love which is to be paid to the physical heart of the Incarnate Word as the symbol of His most ardent love. Even though we must openly admit this, it cannot surprise us nor in any way lead us to doubt that the divine love for us, which is the principal reason for this devotion, is proclaimed and inculcated both in the Old and New Testaments in such vivid images as to greatly stir men's souls. And since these images were presented in the passages of Scripture which announced the coming of the Son of God made man, they can therefore be regarded as a presage of that most excellent sign and symbol of divine love, that is, the most sacred and adorable heart of the divine Redeemer.

LOVE: SEAL OF THE OLD LAW

For our present purpose we do not consider it necessary to cite many passages from the books of the Old Testament, which contain truths revealed by God long ago. We deem it sufficient to recall the covenant which was made between God and the Jewish people and was ratified with peace offerings.

Moses wrote its principal laws on two tables of stone and the prophets expounded them.[16] The covenant was sealed not only by the bonds of God's supreme dominion and the obedience which men owe Him, but was also strengthened and sustained by higher considerations of love.

ISRAEL'S LOVING FEAR

For to the people of Israel the weightiest reason for obeying God was not the fear of divine vengeance, which the thunder and lightning flashing from the peak of Mt. Sinai struck into their souls, but rather the love which they owed God. "Hear, O Israel! The Lord is our God, the Lord alone! Therefore, you shall love the Lord, your God, with all your heart, and with all your soul, and with all your strength. Take to heart these words which I enjoin on you today."[17]

MOSES AND THE PROPHETS

We are not surprised, then, if Moses and the prophets, whom the Angelic Doctor rightly calls the "elders" of the chosen people,[18] because they knew that the foundation of the entire law was placed on this precept of love, described the dealings between God and His people in terms of the mutual love of a father and his children or of a husband and his wife, rather than in stern terms of God's supreme dominion or of our own subjection in fear.

Therefore, to cite a few examples, Moses himself, when he sang his famous canticle because of the liberation of his people from the bondage of Egypt and wanted to declare that it had been accomplished by the power of God, used these touching expressions and comparisons: "As an eagle incites its nestlings forth by hovering over its brood, so he [God] spread his wings to receive them and bore them up on his pinions."[19]

HOSEA: GOD IS A LOVING FATHER

Of the prophets none perhaps more than Hosea expresses and explains so clearly and forcefully the love which God always showed His people. In the writings of this prophet, who is outstanding among the rest of the minor prophets for the austere grandeur of his diction, God manifests a holy and solicitous love for His chosen people, a love like that of a loving and merciful father or that of a husband whose honor is offended.

The sort of love in question here is so far from diminishing or ceasing on account of the perfidy of traitors or enormous crimes, that it will rather justly punish offenses, not indeed to repudiate and dismiss the estranged and faithless wife and ungrateful children, but to make amends and purify and reunite them in renewed and strengthened bonds of love. "Because Israel was a child, and I loved him; and I called my son out of Egypt.... And I was like a foster father to Ephraim, I carried them in my arms; and they knew not that I healed them. I will draw them with the cords of Adam, with the bonds of love.... I will heal their breaches, I will love them freely, for my wrath is turned away from them. I will be as the dew, Israel shall spring as the lily, and his root shall shoot forth as that of Libanus."[20]

ISAIAS...AND THE CANTICLE

The prophet Isaias expresses similar sentiments when he represents God Himself and His chosen people expressing, as it were, opposite views in a conversation: "And Sion said: The Lord has forsaken me, and the Lord has forgotten me. Can a woman forget her infant, so as not to have pity on the son of her womb? And if she should forget, yet will not I forget you."[21]

No less touching are the words which the author of the Canticle of Canticles uses when he graphically describes in terms of conjugal love the bonds of mutual charity which join God and His chosen people: "As the lily among thorns, so is my love among the daughters.... I to my beloved, and my beloved to me, who feeds among the lilies.... Put me as a seal upon your heart, as a seal upon your arm, for love is strong as death, jealousy as hard as hell: the lamps thereof are fire and flames."[22]

HARBINGER OF THE SAVIOR'S LOVE

This most tender, indulgent, and patient love of God, which disclaimed the Jewish people as they added crime upon crime but never completely repudiated them, seems ardent and sublime. But it was only a harbinger of that most ardent love which the Redeemer who had been promised to mankind was to unfold from His most loving heart. This love was to be the exemplar of our love, the foundation of the new covenant. However, only He who is the Only-Begotten of the Father and the Word made flesh "full of grace and of truth,"[23] when He came among men weighed down with countless sins and miseries, could in His human nature, hypostatically united with the divine Person, open for mankind "a fountain of living water" to irrigate the parched earth and transform it into a blooming, fruitful garden.

JEREMIAS' PROPHECY

It seems that the prophet Jeremias in a way foretold that this marvelous transformation would be accomplished through God's most merciful and eternal love, in these words: "I have loved you with an everlasting love, therefore have I drawn you, taking pity.... Behold the days shall come, says the Lord, and I will make a new covenant with the house of Israel, and with the house of Juda.... This shall be the covenant that I will make with the house of Israel, after those days, says the Lord: I will give my law in their bowels, and I will write it in their hearts, and I will be their God, and they shall be my people...for I will forgive their iniquity, and I will remember their sin no more."[24]

II

However, only from the Gospels do we get clear and full knowledge of the new covenant between God and man. The covenant which Moses made between the people of Israel and God was merely the symbol and token which the prophet Jeremias foretold. The real new covenant, we say, is that which was established and accomplished by the Incarnate Word and divine grace reconciling us with God. This covenant must therefore be considered incomparably nobler and more lasting because it was ratified, not by the blood of goats and heifers, as was the first, but by His most holy blood, which the peace offerings—irrational animals—foreshadowed as "the lamb of God, who takes away the sin of the world."[25]

RATIFIED IN FRIENDSHIP

The Christian covenant, much more than the old covenant, clearly shows that it was not based on submission and fear, but ratified in terms of that friendship that must exist between a father and his sons, and sustained and strengthened by a more lavish participation in divine grace and truth, according to the words of St. John the Evangelist: "And of his fullness we have all received, grace for grace. For the Law was given through Moses; grace and truth came through Jesus Christ."[26]

Since we are led, then, to the very mystery of the infinite love of the Incarnate Word by these words of that disciple "whom Jesus loved, the one who, at the supper, had leaned back upon his breast,"[27] it seems meet and just, right and availing unto salvation, venerable brothers, to linger a while in the sweetest contemplation of that mystery, so that, enlightened by the light which shines from the Gospel and sheds light on this mystery, we too may understand and realize the desire expressed by the Apostle of the Gentiles in his letter to the Ephesians: "To have Christ dwelling through faith in your hearts: so that, being rooted and grounded in love, you may be able to comprehend with all the saints what is the breadth and length and height and depth, and to know Christ's love, which surpasses knowledge, in order that you may be filled unto all the fullness of God."[28]

THE REDEMPTION: MYSTERY OF LOVE

The mystery of the divine Redemption is first and foremost a mystery of love, that is, of the true love of Christ for His heavenly Father, to whom the sacrifice offered on the cross in loving obedience renders most abundant and infinite satisfaction for the sins of mankind. "By suffering out of love and obedience, Christ gave more to God than was required to compensate for the offense of the whole human race."[29] It is, moreover, a mystery of the merciful love of the august Trinity and the divine Redeemer for all mankind. Since men could not possibly make adequate expiation for their sins,[30] Christ, through the unfathomable riches of the merits which He acquired for us by shedding His precious blood, was able to restore and perfect the bond of friendship between God and men which had been severed first in paradise by the pitiful fall of Adam, and later by the countless sins of the chosen people.

GOD'S JUSTICE AND MERCY

Therefore the divine Redeemer, as our duly constituted and perfect Mediator, because He made perfect satisfaction to divine justice for all the debts and obligations of the human race out of His most ardent love for us, effected the marvelous reconciliation between divine justice and divine mercy which constitutes the unsurpassed mystery of our salvation.

Concerning this mystery, the Angelic Doctor wisely says:

"That man should be delivered by Christ's passion was in keeping with both His mercy and His justice. With His justice, because by His passion Christ made satisfaction for the sin of the human race; and so man was set free by Christ's justice: and with His mercy, for since man of himself could not satisfy for the sin of all human nature God gave him His Son to satisfy for him.

"And this came of a more copious mercy than if He had forgiven sins without satisfaction. Hence St. Paul says: 'God, who is rich in mercy, by reason of his very great love wherewith he has loved us, when we were dead by reason of our sins, brought us to life together with Christ.'"[31]

DIVINE AND HUMAN LOVE OF CHRIST

However, that we may be able, so far as it is possible for mortal man "to comprehend with all the saints what is the breadth and length and height and depth"[32] of the sacred love of the Incarnate Word for His heavenly Father and for men defiled by sin, we must understand that His love was not solely the spiritual love which is proper to God because "God is Spirit."[33] To be sure, the love with which God loved our first parents and the Hebrew people was of this spiritual nature. The expressions of love, so human, intimate and paternal, which we read in the Psalms, in the writings of the prophets and in the Canticle of Canticles, are indications and manifestations of the most genuine but entirely spiritual love with which God loved the human race. On the contrary, the love spoken of in the Gospel, the letters of the apostles and the pages of the book of Revelation—all of which describe the love of the heart of Jesus Christ—express not only divine love but also human sentiments of love.

PERFECT GOD AND PERFECT MAN

This point is quite clear to all who are Catholics. For the Word of God assumed not a fictitious and empty body, as was asserted in the first century of the Christian era by some heretics who were condemned by St. John the apostle in most severe terms: "For many deceivers have gone forth into the world, who do not confess Jesus as the Christ coming in the flesh. This is the deceiver and the Antichrist."[34] But the Word actually united to His divine Person an individual, integral and perfect human nature which was conceived by the power of the Holy Spirit in the most pure womb of the Virgin Mary.[35] Nothing, therefore, was lacking in the human nature which the Word of God joined to Himself. Indeed He assumed a human nature in no way diminished or changed in its spiritual and bodily capacities, that is, a nature endowed with intelligence and will and the other internal and external faculties of perception, with sense appetites and all the natural impulses.

The Catholic Church teaches all these doctrines as solemnly proclaimed and confirmed by the Roman Pontiffs and general councils: "Whole and entire in what is His own, whole and entire in what is ours"[36]; "perfect in His Godhead and likewise perfect in His humanity"[37]; "complete God is man, complete man is God."[38]

THE THREEFOLD LOVE OF CHRIST

Therefore, there can be no doubt that Jesus Christ took a real body having all the affections which are proper to it, among which love certainly holds the first place. Likewise, therefore, there can be no doubt that He had a physical heart like ours, since without this most excellent organ human life, and certainly where affections are concerned, is impossible. Wherefore, the heart of Jesus Christ, hypostatically united to the divine Person of the Word, beyond doubt throbbed with love and the rest of the impulses of the affections which, however, were in such perfect accord and harmony with His human will, filled with divine love and with the infinite love itself which the Son shares with the Father and the Holy Spirit, that there never was any contradiction or conflict between these three loves.[39]

The Word of God took upon Himself a real and perfect human nature and formed and fashioned for Himself a heart of flesh, which, like ours, could suffer and be pierced. And yet, unless this teaching be considered not only in the light which is shed by the hypostatic and substantial union, but also in that of the redemption of mankind—its complement, as it were—it can be a stumbling block and foolishness to some, as Christ nailed to the cross actually was to the Jews and Gentiles.[40]

The authoritative teaching of the Catholic Faith, in complete agreement with Holy Scripture, assures us that a human nature capable of suffering and dying was assumed by the only-begotten Son of God precisely because He wished to offer the bloody sacrifice on the cross in order to accomplish the task of man's redemption.

"LIKE UNTO HIS BRETHREN"

The Apostle of the Gentiles teaches this doctrine under another aspect in these words: "For both he who sanctifies and they who are sanctified are all from one. For which cause he is not ashamed to call them brethren, saying, 'I will declare your name to my brethren....' And again, 'Behold, I and my children, whom God has given me.' Therefore, because children have blood and flesh in common, so he in like manner has shared in these.... Wherefore it was right that he should in all things be made like unto his brethren, that he might become a merciful and faithful high priest before God to expiate the sins of the people. For in that he himself has suffered and has been tempted, he is able to help those who are tempted."[41]

WITNESS OF THE FATHERS

The Fathers of the Church, truthful witnesses of divinely revealed doctrine, understood most definitely what the Apostle Paul had quite clearly stated: that the mysteries of the Incarnation and Redemption were the beginning and culmination of divine love. Frequently, and in clear words, we read in their writings that Jesus Christ assumed perfect human nature and our mortal and perishable body, to provide for our eternal salvation and to show us His infinite, even sensible, love.

THE GREEK FATHERS

Echoing the words of the Apostle of the Gentiles, St. Justin writes: "We adore and love the Word born of the unbegotten and ineffable God since He became Man for our sake, so that having become partaker of our sufferings He might provide a remedy for them."[42] St. Basil, first of the three Cappadocian Fathers, teaches that the affections of the senses in Christ were at one and the same time real and holy. "It is clear that the Lord did indeed assume natural affections as a proof of His real and not imaginary Incarnation and that He rejected as unworthy of the Godhead corrupt affections which defile the purity of our life."[43] In like manner, the light of the church of Antioch, St. John Chrysostom, states that the affections of the senses to which the divine Redeemer was susceptible prove beyond doubt that He assumed a complete human nature. "For if He had not shared our nature, He would not have repeatedly been seized with grief."[44]

ST. AMBROSE AND ST. JEROME

Of the Latin Fathers we select for mention those whom the Church today honors as Doctors. St. Ambrose testifies that the movement of the senses and the affections which Christ truly experienced are rooted in the hypostatic union as in a natural principle: "And therefore He assumed a soul and the passions of the soul; for God, precisely because He is God, could not have been disturbed nor could He have died."[45]

From these affections St. Jerome draws his chief proof that Christ assumed human nature: To prove that He really assumed human nature, He really became sorrowful.[46] St. Augustine in a special manner calls attention to the relationship between the affections of the Incarnate Word and the purpose of the redemption of the human race: "These affections of human infirmity, just as the very flesh of human infirmity and the death of human flesh, the Lord Jesus assumed not out of necessity but freely out of compassion so that He might transform in Himself His body, which is the Church of which He deigned to be the Head, that is, His members in the faithful and the saints, so that if any of them in the trials of this life should be saddened and afflicted, they should not therefore think that they are deprived of His grace; nor should they consider this sorrow a sin, but a sign of human weakness; like a choir singing in harmony with the note that has been sounded, so should His body learn from its Head."[47]

ST. JOHN DAMASCENE

In less ornate but nevertheless forceful words, the following passages from St. John Damascene set forth the clear teaching of the Church: "Complete God took me up completely, and whole was united to whole, that He might bestow salvation upon the whole. For what was not assumed could not be healed."[48] "He therefore assumed all that He might sanctify all."[49]

We must, however, bear in mind that these quotations from Scripture and the Fathers and not a few similar ones which we did not cite, although they clearly attest that there were in Jesus Christ movements of the senses and affections and that He assumed human nature to accomplish our eternal salvation, never refer these affections to His physical heart in such a manner as to indicate it clearly as the symbol of His infinite love.

THE SAVIOR'S COUNTENANCE

But if the evangelists and the rest of the sacred writers do not clearly describe the heart of our Redeemer as responding to feelings and emotions no less than ours and as throbbing and palpitating on account of the various movements and affections of His soul and of the most ardent love of His human and divine wills, nonetheless they frequently do clearly record His divine love and those movements of the emotions connected with it, namely, desire, joy, sadness, fear and anger as they are reflected in His countenance, words and manner of acting.

Our adorable Savior's face was an indication and perfect mirror of those affections which moved His soul in various ways and, by a sort of sympathetic vibration, touched His Sacred Heart and set it beating. The observation which the Angelic Doctor drew from common experience concerning human psychology and its consequences is pertinent to this matter: "The disturbance of anger reaches to the outward members and chiefly to those members which reflect more distinctly the emotions of the heart, such as the eyes, face and tongue."[50]

THE HEART: INDEX OF CHRIST'S THREEFOLD LOVE

Wherefore the heart of the Incarnate Word is rightly considered the chief index and symbol of the threefold love with which the divine Redeemer continuously loves the eternal Father and the whole human race. It is the symbol of that divine love which He shares with the Father and the Holy

Spirit, but which in Him alone, in the Word namely that was made flesh, is manifested to us through a frail, mortal, human body, since "in him dwells the fullness of the Godhead bodily."[51]

It is moreover the symbol of that most ardent love which, infused into His soul, enriches the human will of Christ, and whose action is enlightened and directed by a twofold most perfect knowledge, namely, the beatific and infused.[52]

Finally, in a more direct and natural manner, it is a symbol also of sensible love, since the body of Jesus Christ, formed through the operation of the Holy Spirit in the womb of the Virgin Mary, has a most perfect capacity for feeling and perception, much more than the bodies of all other men.[53]

VENERATION DUE THE SACRED HEART

Since Scripture and the teachings of the Catholic Faith affirm that there is the highest possible harmony and agreement in the most holy soul of Jesus Christ, and that He clearly directed His threefold love to accomplish our redemption, it is therefore obvious that we can most correctly consider and venerate the heart of the divine Redeemer as the significant image of His love, the proof of our redemption, and the mystical ladder by which we climb to the embrace of "God our Savior."[54]

Wherefore His words, actions, teachings, miracles, and in particular those deeds which more clearly testify this love for us—the institution of the Holy Eucharist, His most bitter passion and death, His most holy Mother whom He lovingly gave to us, the founding of the Church, and the sending of the Holy Spirit upon the apostles and upon us—all these we must regard as proofs of His threefold love.

MEDITATE THIS HEART

In like manner we must lovingly meditate on the pulsations of His Sacred Heart by which, so to speak, He Himself seemed to measure the time of His sojourn on earth up to that last moment when, as the evangelists testify, "crying out in a loud voice, 'It is consummated,' and, bowing his head, he gave up his spirit."[55]

Then the beating of His heart stopped, and His sensible love was interrupted until He arose from the tomb in triumph over death.

But after His glorified body was again united to the soul of the divine Redeemer, the conqueror of death, His Sacred Heart never ceased, and never will cease, to beat with imperturbable and calm pulsation. It will likewise never cease to signify His threefold love by which the Son of God is bound to His heavenly Father and the whole human race, of which He is by perfect right the mystical Head.

III

But now, venerable brothers, in order that we may gather rich and salutary fruits from these pious considerations, let us briefly meditate on and contemplate the manifold affections, human and divine, of our Savior, Jesus Christ, which His heart manifested through the course of His mortal life, manifests now, and will continue to manifest forever. Especially from the pages of the Gospel does light shine forth to us. Illumined and strengthened by this light, we can enter into the tabernacle of His divine heart. Together with the Apostle of the Gentiles we can wonder at "the riches of grace in kindness towards us in Christ Jesus."[56]

THE INCARNATION

The adorable heart of Jesus Christ beats with human and divine love since the Virgin Mary pronounced that great-souled "*Fiat*" and the Word of God, as the Apostle observes, "coming into the world, says, *Sacrifice and oblation you would not, but a body you have fitted to me: in holocausts and sin-offerings you have had no pleasure. Then said I, 'Behold, I come'*.... It is in this 'will' that we have been sanctified through the offering of the body of Jesus Christ once for all."[57]

THE HOME AND SHOP AT NAZARETH

In the same way was He moved by love in perfect accord with the affections of His human will and divine love when in the home at Nazareth He engaged in heavenly discourse with His most sweet Mother and His foster father, Joseph, with whom He toiled obediently in the carpenter's trade. With the threefold love of which we have spoken, He was driven on during the lengthy apostolic journeys which He undertook, in the innumerable miracles which He wrought and by which He recalled the dead from the tomb or bestowed health on those ill with every sort of disease. He was moved by this threefold love during the labors He endured and in the sweat, hunger and thirst He suffered and in the nocturnal vigils in which He most lovingly prayed to His heavenly Father.

HIS PARABLES

And finally He was moved by this threefold love in the discourses He delivered and in the parables which He spoke and explained, in those for instance, which treat of His mercy, such as the parables of the lost drachma, the lost sheep, the prodigal son. In these parables, both by their subject matter and by words, the very heart of God is expressly laid bare to us, as Gregory the Great observed: "Learn of the heart of God in the words of God, so that you may more ardently long for eternal things."[58]

HIS WORDS OF LOVE

But the heart of Christ was moved by an even greater charity when words full of love fell from His lips. Let us cite some examples. When He saw the crowds tired and hungry, He exclaimed, "I have compassion on the crowd."[59] And when He gazed upon Jerusalem, His most beloved city, blinded by her sins and therefore destined for complete destruction, He said: "Jerusalem, Jerusalem! You who kill the prophets, and stone those who are sent to you! How often would I have gathered your children together, as a hen gathers her young under her wings, but you would not!"[60]

LOVING INDIGNATION

But, because of love for His Father and holy indignation, His heart beat violently when He beheld the sacrilegious buying and selling in the temple, and He rebuked the profaners of the temple with these words: "It is written, 'My house shall be called a house of prayer; but you have made it a den of thieves.'"[61]

IN THE GARDEN OF GETHSEMANE

But His heart was moved by a special love and fear when He saw that the hour of His most cruel sufferings was now at hand. He felt a natural repugnance for death and those sorrows which were rushing upon Him, and cried out: "Father, if it is possible, let this cup pass away from me."[62]

But when He received a kiss from the traitor, it was with unconquered love and the deepest grief that He addressed him in these words which seem to be the last invitation of His most merciful heart to a friend who, with an impious, faithless and most hardened heart, was about to betray Him to His executioners: "Friend, for what purpose have you come? Do you betray the Son of Man with a kiss?"[63]

THE DAUGHTERS OF JERUSALEM

But He spoke with exceedingly great love and pity when He said to the pious women weeping for Him as He was about to suffer the undeserved death of the cross: "Daughters of Jerusalem, do not weep for me, but weep for yourselves and for your children.... For if in the case of green wood they do these things, what is to happen in the case of the dry?"[64]

ON THE CROSS

And finally, our divine Redeemer, hanging on the cross, felt His heart on fire with varied and vehement affections of the most ardent love, of dismay, of mercy, of most intense longing, of serene calm, affections which are indeed most strikingly expressed by the following words: "Father, forgive them, for they do not know what they are doing."[65] "My God, my God, why have you forsaken me?"[66] "Amen I say to you, this day you shall be with me in paradise."[67] "I thirst."[68] "Father, into your hands I commend my spirit."[69]

HIS GREATEST GIFTS

Who in truth could worthily describe those beatings of the divine heart, the indications of His infinite love, which He elicited at those moments when He bestowed His greatest gifts on man, that is, Himself in the sacrament of the Eucharist, His most holy Mother, and the priestly office which is shared with us?

THE HOLY EUCHARIST

Even before He ate the Last Supper with His disciples, when He knew that He was going to institute the sacrament of His body and blood by the shedding of which the new covenant was to be consecrated, He felt His heart stirred by strong emotions, which He made known to the apostles in these words: "I have greatly desired to eat this passover with you before I suffer."[70] These same emotions were even stronger, without doubt, when "having taken bread, he gave thanks and broke it and gave it to them, saying: 'This is my body which is being given for you; do this in remembrance of me.' In like manner, he took also the cup after the supper, saying: 'This cup is the new covenant in my blood, which shall be shed for you.'"[71]

Rightly, therefore, one may affirm that the divine Eucharist, both as a sacrament and as a sacrifice—the one He bestowed on men, the other He Himself continually offers "from the rising of the sun even to the going down,"[72]—and the priesthood are really gifts of the Sacred Heart of Jesus.

MOTHER OF GOD AND MANKIND

Indeed another most precious gift of His Sacred Heart is, as we have said, Mary, the sweet Mother of God and the most loving Mother of us all. For she was the Mother of our Redeemer according to the flesh and His associate in recalling the children of Eve to the life of divine grace. And so she is rightly hailed as the spiritual Mother of mankind. Wherefore St. Augustine in writing of her says:

"Indeed she is the Mother of the members of the Savior, which we are, because she cooperated by love so that the faithful who are the members of that Head might be born in the Church."[73]

THE BLOODY SACRIFICE

And to the unbloody gift of Himself, under the appearance of bread and wine, our Savior, Jesus Christ, wished, as a special proof of His intimate and infinite love, to add the bloody sacrifice of the cross. Indeed, in this way of acting, He gave an example of that sublime charity which He set before His disciples as the highest measure of love: "Greater love than this no one has, that one lay down his life for his friends."[74]

Wherefore, the love of Jesus Christ, the Son of God, by the sacrifice of Golgotha, clearly and richly proves the love of God Himself: "In this we have come to know his love, that he laid down his life for us; and we likewise ought to lay down our life for the brethren."[75]

And in fact our divine Redeemer was nailed to the cross more by His love than by the force of the executioners. His voluntary holocaust is the supreme gift which He bestowed on each man according to the concise words of the Apostle: "Who loved me, and gave himself up for me."[76]

MYSTICAL MARRIAGE OF SAVIOR AND CHURCH

Therefore, there can be no doubt that the Sacred Heart of Jesus, since it shares most intimately in the life of the Incarnate Word, and was therefore assumed as an instrument of the Godhead no less than were the other members of His human nature in accomplishing the works of divine grace and omnipotence,[77] is the true symbol of the boundless love by which our Savior, through the shedding of His blood, contracted a mystical marriage with the Church. "Through charity He suffered for the Church who was to be united to Him as His spouse."[78]

THE CHURCH BORN OF CHRIST'S LOVE

Therefore, from the wounded heart of our Redeemer, the Church, the dispenser of the blood of the Redeemer, was born. From this same heart the grace of the sacraments, from which the children of the Church draw supernatural life, flowed most profusely, as we read in the sacred liturgy: "From the pierced heart, the Church, joined to Christ, is born...who pours forth grace from Your heart."[79] On the meaning of this symbol, which was not unknown even to the ancient Fathers of the Church and ecclesiastical writers, the Angelic Doctor, as if re-echoing their very sentiments, writes: "Water flowed from Christ's side to wash us; blood, to redeem us. Wherefore blood belongs to the sacrament of the Eucharist, while water belongs to the sacrament of Baptism. Yet this latter sacrament derives its cleaning virtue from the power of Christ's blood."[80]

THE WOUNDED SIDE

What is written here concerning the side of Christ, wounded and opened by a soldier, must likewise be said of His heart, which the lance certainly touched in its thrust, inasmuch as the soldier pierced it in order to be certain that Jesus Christ had died upon the cross.

Wherefore the wound of the Sacred Heart of Jesus, which had now completed this mortal life, has been through the ages a living image of that love freely bestowed by which God gave His only-begotten Son for the redemption of man, and with which Christ loved us all so intensely that He offered Himself for us as a bloody victim on Calvary: "Christ also loved us and delivered himself up for us as an offering and a sacrifice to God to ascend in fragrant odor."[81]

CHRIST'S LOVE FOR THE CHURCH

After our Savior ascended into heaven—His body adorned with the splendor of eternal glory—and sat at the right hand of the Father, He did not cease to bestow upon His spouse, the Church, that ardent love with which His heart beats. Indeed in His hands and feet and side He bears the glowing marks of the wounds which represent the triple victory gained by Him over the devil, sin and death.

He likewise has in His heart, placed, as it were, in a most precious shrine, those treasures of merit, the fruits of His triple triumph. These He bestows generously on redeemed mankind. This is a truth full of consolation, which the Apostle of the Gentiles stated in these words: "Ascending on high, he led away captives; he gave gifts to men. He who descended, he it is who ascended also above all the heavens, that he might fill all things."[82]

THE PARACLETE

The gift of the Holy Spirit, sent to the disciples, is the first clear sign of His munificent charity after His triumphal ascent to the right hand of the Father. Indeed after ten days the Spirit, the Paraclete, given by the heavenly Father, descended upon them gathered in the Cenacle, as He had promised them at the Last Supper: "I will ask the Father and he will give you another Advocate to dwell with you forever."[83]

This Spirit, the Paraclete, since He is the personified mutual love of the Father for the Son and of the Son for the Father, is sent indeed by both. Assuming the appearance of tongues of fire, He poured the abundance of divine love and other heavenly gifts into their souls. The infusion of this divine love also sprang from the heart of our Savior, "in whom are hidden all the treasures of wisdom and knowledge."[84]

THE GIFT OF CHARITY

Indeed, this love is the gift of the heart of Jesus and His Spirit, who is indeed the Spirit of the Father and the Son, and from whom both the rise of the Church and its remarkable spread are unfolded for all the pagan nations, which the worship of idols, hatred of brothers, corruption of morals, and violence had befouled.

APOSTLES, MARTYRS AND DOCTORS

This divine love is the most precious gift of the heart of Christ and of His Spirit. It gave the apostles and martyrs that fortitude with which they were strengthened to fight even to the point of death, which they met with heroic spirit, to preach the truth of the Gospel and to bear witness by the shedding of their blood. It gave the Doctors of the Church a most ardent desire to teach and defend the Catholic Faith.

CONFESSORS, VIRGINS, ALL THE FAITHFUL

It was this love which nourished the virtues of the confessors and urged them to accomplish eminently useful and marvelous deeds, profitable for their own eternal and temporal welfare and that of others. This was the love which persuaded virgins to abstain, willingly and joyfully, from the pleasures of the senses, and to consecrate themselves entirely to the love of their heavenly Spouse.

THE HYMN OF ST. PAUL

In praise of this divine love which flows from the heart of the Incarnate Word and is infused by the operation of the Holy Spirit in the souls of all the faithful, the Apostle of the Gentiles wrote the famous hymn of victory which proclaims the triumph of Jesus Christ and the members of the Mystical Body, of which He is the Head, over all obstacles to restoring the reign of divine love among men: "Who shall separate us from the love of Christ? Shall tribulation, or distress, or persecution, or hunger, or nakedness, or danger, or the sword? But in all these things we overcome because of him who has loved us. For I am sure that neither death, nor life, nor angels, nor principalities, nor things present, nor things to come, nor powers, nor height, nor depth, nor any other creature will be able to separate us from the love of God which is in Christ Jesus our Lord."[85]

THE LIVING HEART

There is nothing, then, which forbids us to adore the most Sacred Heart of Jesus, since it participates in and is the natural and most expressive symbol of that inexhaustible love with which our divine Redeemer still loves mankind. That heart indeed, although it is no longer liable to the disturbances of this mortal life, still lives and beats. It is now inseparably joined with the Person of the divine Word, and in it and through it with His divine will.

Wherefore, since the heart of Christ overflows with divine and human love, and since it is abundantly rich with treasures of all the graces which our Redeemer acquired by His life, His sufferings, and death, it is truly the unfailing fountain of that love which His Spirit pours forth into all the members of His Mystical Body.

IMAGE OF THE DIVINE PERSON

Therefore the heart of our Savior in a way expresses the image of the divine Person of the Word and His twofold nature, human and divine. In it we can contemplate not only the symbol, but also, as it were, the sum of the whole mystery of our redemption.

When we adore the Sacred Heart of Jesus Christ, we adore in it and through it both the uncreated love of the divine Word and His human love and other affections and virtues, because both loves moved our Redeemer to sacrifice Himself for us and for the whole Church, His Spouse. As the Apostle says: "Christ also loved the Church and delivered himself up for her, that he might sanctify her, cleansing her in the bath of water by means of the word, in order that he might present to himself the Church in all her glory, not having spot or wrinkle or any such thing, but that she might be holy and without blemish."[86]

As Christ loved the Church, so He still loves her most deeply with that threefold love of which we have spoken. This love moves Him as our advocate[87] to win grace and mercy for us from the Father, "since he lives always to make intercession for us."[88] The prayers which come forth from His inexhaustible love and which are directed to the Father are never interrupted. As "in the days of his earthly life,"[89] so now, triumphant in heaven, He beseeches the Father with no less efficacy.

He shows His living heart to Him who "so loved the world that he gave his only-begotten Son, that those who believe in him may not perish, but may have life everlasting."[90] His heart is, as it were, wounded and burning with even greater love than when it was pierced after death by the lance of a Roman soldier. "Wherefore [Your heart] was wounded so that through the visible wound we might see the invisible wound of love."[91]

It is then absolutely certain that the heavenly Father "who has not spared even his own Son, but has delivered him for us all,"[92] when He has been asked by so powerful an Advocate and with such ardent love, will always send down a rich flow of divine graces to all men.

IV

It has been our wish, venerable brothers, to explain to you and all Christians, in summary fashion, the real nature of devotion to the Sacred Heart of Jesus and the endless riches which flow from it, as they have been made known in Divine Revelation, as in a primary source.

We think that our statements, confirmed by the teaching of the Gospel, have made it clear that essentially this devotion is nothing else than devotion to the human and divine love of the Incarnate Word and to the love which the heavenly Father and the Holy Spirit have for sinful men.

LOVE: FIRST CAUSE OF OUR REDEMPTION

For, as the Angelic Doctor teaches, the love of the august Trinity is the first cause of man's redemption in that, pouring forth abundantly into the human will of Jesus Christ and into His adorable heart, it led Him, moved by that selfsame love, to the shedding of His blood to redeem us from the captivity of sin.[93] "I have a baptism to be baptized with; and how distressed I am until it is accomplished!"[94]

We know, therefore, that the devotion whereby we pay homage to the love of God and Jesus Christ for men through the august sign of the wounded heart of the Redeemer nailed to the cross has never been entirely unknown to Christian piety. In more recent times, however, this devotion has become better known and wondrously spread throughout the Church, particularly after the Lord Himself privately revealed this divine secret to some of His children, richly endowed with an abundance of heavenly gifts, and chose them as the messengers and heralds of this devotion.

Indeed, there always have been souls especially dedicated to God, who, imitating the example of the holy Mother of God, the apostles and the illustrious Fathers of the Church, have adored, thanked and loved Christ's most sacred human nature, especially the wounds inflicted on His body during His salutary passion.

CONFESSION OF THOMAS THE APOSTLE

Furthermore, do not these very words, "My Lord and my God,"[95] spoken by the Apostle Thomas and which signified that he had been changed from an unbeliever into a faithful follower, contain a clear profession of faith, adoration and love rising from the wounded humanity of the Lord to the majesty of the divine Person?

GRADUAL GROWTH OF THE DEVOTION

But if men were always strongly moved by the wounded heart of the Redeemer to venerate the infinite love with which He loves the human race, since the words of the prophet Zacharias, applied by St. John the Evangelist to Christ on the cross, "They shall look upon him whom they have pierced,"[96] were addressed to the faithful of all ages, we must nevertheless admit that only gradually and by degrees was the homage of special devotion paid to His heart as the image of the human and divine love dwelling in the Incarnate Word.

A DEVOTION FOSTERED BY GOD'S SAINTS

If we wish to sketch the significant stages, as it were, in the progress of this devotion in the history of piety, there immediately come to mind the names of some who have gained special renown in this respect and who are to be considered the standard-bearers of this devotion which gradually gained momentum privately in religious communities.

We mention, by way of example, the names of those who achieved special distinction in establishing and promoting devotion to the most Sacred Heart of Jesus: St. Bonaventure, St. Albert the Great, St. Gertrude, St. Catherine of Siena, Blessed Henry Suso, St. Peter Canisius, St. Francis de Sales and St. John Eudes, author of the first liturgical office to be celebrated in honor of the most Sacred Heart of Jesus.

With the approval of many bishops of France, this solemn feast was celebrated for the first time on October 20, 1672.

ST. MARGARET MARY

Among those who have promoted this most excellent devotion, St. Margaret Mary Alacoque occupies the chief place of honor. Inflamed with great zeal and with the aid of her spiritual director, Blessed Claude de la Colombière, she succeeded in her efforts, to the great wonder of the faithful, to have this devotion, rich in spiritual blessings, established and clearly distinguished from other forms of Christian piety by the special nature of its acts of love and reparation.[97]

NOT BECAUSE PRIVATELY REVEALED

A review of the history of the period in which this devotion to the Sacred Heart of Jesus developed is enough to increase our clear understanding that its marvelous progress is due to the fact that this devotion is in perfect accord with the nature of the Christian religion, which is indeed a religion of love.

Therefore, we must not say that this devotion began because it was privately revealed by God or that it suddenly came into existence in the Church, but rather that it is the spontaneous flowering of a living faith and fervent piety by which men filled with supernatural gifts were led to adore the Redeemer and His glorious wounds as symbols of His boundless love which stirred their souls to the very depths.

CHRIST'S WISH AND CALL

Consequently, as is obvious, the revelations made to Saint Margaret Mary added nothing new to Catholic doctrine. The significance of these revelations lies in this, that Christ the Lord – showing His Sacred Heart – willed in an extraordinary and special way to call the minds of men to the contemplation and veneration of the mystery of God's most merciful love for the human race.

And so in this special manifestation, in repeated and clear words, Christ pointed to His heart as the symbol by which men are drawn to recognize and acknowledge His love, and at the same time constituted it as the sign and pledge of His mercy and His grace for the needs of the Church in our time.

THE LITURGICAL FEAST

Moreover, the fact that this devotion stems from the principles of Christian doctrine is clearly demonstrated by the fact that the Apostolic See approved the liturgical feast before it approved the writings of St. Margaret Mary. For, not strictly basing their action on any private divine revelation, but graciously granting the petitions of the faithful, the Sacred Congregation of Rites in a decree of January 25, 1765, approved by our predecessor, Clement XIII, on February 6 of the same year, granted the celebration of a liturgical feast to the bishops of Poland and to the Roman Archconfraternity of the Sacred Heart.

The Apostolic See granted this petition to extend an already existing and flourishing devotion, whose purpose was "symbolically to renew the memory of that divine love"[98] by which our Redeemer was impelled to offer Himself as a propitiatory victim for the crimes of men.

This first approbation was granted in the form of a privilege and was restricted to definite regions. After almost a century, another approbation followed of far greater importance, and phrased in more solemn words. We are referring, as we previously mentioned, to the decree of the Sacred Congregation of Rites issued August 23, 1856. By it our predecessor of immortal memory, Pius IX, acceding to the petitions of the bishops of France and of almost the whole Catholic world, ordered the feast of the Sacred Heart of Jesus to be extended to the entire Church and to be duly celebrated.[99] The faithful should always remember this decree, for, as we read in the liturgy of this feast, "Since that time devotion to the most Sacred Heart, gushing forth like a mighty stream, has spread throughout the world, washing away every obstacle in its course."

From the explanations which we have thus far given, venerable brothers, it is perfectly clear that the faithful must trace devotion to the Sacred Heart of Jesus back to Sacred Scripture, tradition and the liturgy, as to a clear and deep fountain, if they wish to understand its real meaning and, through pious meditation, receive food to nourish and increase their religious fervor.

THE ACME OF CHRISTIAN LIFE

If this devotion is constantly practiced with this knowledge and understanding, the souls of the faithful cannot but attain to the sweet knowledge of the love of Christ which produces the height of Christian life, as the Apostle, who knew this from personal experience, teaches: "For this reason I bend my knees to the Father of our Lord Jesus Christ...that he may grant you from his glorious riches to be strengthened with power through his Spirit unto the progress of the inner man; and to have Christ dwelling through faith in your hearts: so that, being rooted and grounded in love, you may be able...to know Christ's love which surpasses knowledge, in order that you may be filled unto all the fullness of God."[100]

THE GOODNESS AND KINDNESS OF GOD

The heart of Christ is the clearest image of this fullness of God embracing all things. By this we mean the fullness of mercy which is the special characteristic of the New Testament, in which "the goodness and kindness of God our Savior appeared."[101] "For God did not send his Son into the world in order to judge the world, but that the world might be saved through him."[102]

POISON OF MATERIALISM AND SUPERSTITION

From the very day on which she issued the first decree concerning devotion to the Sacred Heart of Jesus, the Church, the teacher of mankind, has always been certain that the essential characteristics of this devotion—that is, acts of love and reparation by which God's infinite love for mankind is venerated—are in no way infected with the poison of *materialism* or superstition.

On the contrary, the Church holds that this devotion is a form of piety by which is accomplished a religious worship pertaining to the Spirit and perfectly true, which the Savior Himself foretold in His conversation with the Samaritan woman: "But the hour is coming, and is now here, when the true worshippers will worship the Father in spirit and in truth. For the Father also seeks such to worship him. God is spirit, and they who worship him must worship in spirit and in truth."[103]

A FALSE MYSTICISM

It is therefore wrong to say that contemplation of the physical heart of Jesus is a hindrance to attaining intimate love of God, and that it impedes the soul in its progress to the highest virtues.

The Church completely condemns this false mysticism, just as she did when she spoke through our predecessor of happy memory, Innocent XI, who condemned the errors of those who idly maintained: "Nor must they [souls of the interior way] elicit acts of love for the Blessed Virgin, or the saints or the humanity of Christ for, since these are sensible objects, love for them is of the same nature. No creature, neither the Blessed Virgin nor the saints, must have a place in our heart, because God wishes to occupy and possess it."[104]

THE WORSHIP PAID TO IMAGES

It is evident that those who hold such opinions think that the image of the heart of Christ represents nothing nobler than His sensible love and that this image is not of such a nature as to be a new basis for adoration [*cultus latriae*], which is given only to that which is by its nature divine.

There is no one who does not see that this interpretation of sacred images is entirely false since it confines their meaning, which is much broader, within too narrow limits. Catholic theologians hold and teach a contrary doctrine, and among them St. Thomas has this to say: "The worship of religion is paid to images not as considered in themselves, nor as things, but as images leading us to God Incarnate. Now, movement to an image does not stop at the image, but goes on to the thing it represents. Hence, neither latria nor the virtue of religion is differentiated by the fact that religious worship is paid to the images of Christ."[105]

FROM THE SYMBOL TO THE SYMBOLIZED

The veneration paid to His images, the excellence of which must be determined by what is venerated, or to relics of the bitter sufferings which our Savior endured for us, or to the picture of the pierced heart of Christ hanging on the cross, which surpasses everything in force and meaning, is paid to the very Person of the Incarnate Word as its final object.

Therefore, from the physical thing which the heart of Jesus Christ is, and from its natural symbolism, it is right and proper that, supported by Christian faith, we not only rise to contemplate His love which is perceived through the senses, but go even higher to consider and adore the sublime infused love, and finally, by some sweet and sublime ascent of the spirit, rise to meditate on and adore the divine love of the Incarnate Word.

PHYSICAL HEART AND SPIRITUAL LOVE

For by faith, through which we believe that the human and the divine nature were united in the Person of Christ, we can see the closest bonds between the sensible love of the physical heart of Jesus and the twofold spiritual love, namely, human and divine.

We must say not only that these loves were simultaneously present in the adorable Person of the divine Redeemer, but also that they were joined by a natural bond so that the human and sensible loves are subject to the divine and bear its analogical resemblance. We do not, however, maintain that the heart of Jesus is to be understood in such a way that in it we have and adore a formal image, as it is called, or a perfect and absolute sign of His divine love, since the essence of this love can in no way be adequately expressed by any created image whatsoever.

But the Christian, in honoring the heart of Jesus, adores, together with the Church, the sign and manifestation of divine love, which went so far as to love through the heart of the Incarnate Word the human race defiled with countless sins.

BASIS: THE HYPOSTATIC UNION

It is therefore necessary, at this central point of a teaching which is so important and profound, that everyone bear in mind that the truth of the natural symbol by which the physical heart of Jesus is referred to the Person of the Word rests completely on the fundamental doctrine of the hypostatic union.

If anyone were to deny that this doctrine is true, he would renew false teachings which deny that there is one Person in Christ with two distinct and complete natures; these teachings have been repeatedly condemned by the Church.

With this fundamental truth firmly established, we understand that the heart of Jesus is the heart of a divine Person, that is, of the Incarnate Word, and that by it all the love with which He loved, and even now continues to love us, is represented and, so to speak, placed before our very eyes.

A PERFECT PROFESSION OF THE CHRISTIAN RELIGION

Therefore, devotion to the Sacred Heart is so important that it may be considered, so far as practice is concerned, a perfect profession of the Christian religion.

For this is the religion of Jesus, which rests entirely on a Mediator who is man and God, so that no one can come to the heart of God except through the heart of Christ, as He Himself says: "I am the way, and the truth, and the life. No one comes to the Father but through me."[106]

ADORATION, THANKSGIVING, IMITATION

Since this is true, we readily understand that devotion to the Sacred Heart of Jesus is essentially devotion to the love with which God loved us through Jesus and is at the same time an enlivening of our love for God and man. Or, to put it in other words, this devotion is directed to God's love for us in order to adore Him, to thank Him and to spend our lives imitating Him.

THE NEW COMMANDMENT

It looks toward this as its goal, that we bring the love by which we are bound to God and our fellow men to perfection, by daily observing more eagerly the *new* commandment which the Divine Master gave to His disciples as a sacred inheritance when He said: "A new commandment I give you, that you love one another as I have loved you.... This is my commandment, that you love one another as I have loved you."[107]

This commandment is indeed *new* and Christ's *very own.* As St. Thomas says, "The difference between the Old and New Testaments is told in a few words, for as Jeremias says, 'I will make a new covenant with the house of Israel.'[108] However, because the commandment was in the Old Testament through fear and holy love, it related to the New Testament: hence this commandment was in the old law not as something that belonged to it but as a preparation for the new law."[109]

V

We have presented for your consideration the real nature and excellence of this kind of devotion—beautiful teachings filled with consolation. But before we close this letter, mindful of the Apostolic office, which was first entrusted to St. Peter after his threefold protestation of love for Christ the Lord, we deem it fitting to exhort you again, venerable brothers, and through you all of our dearly beloved children in Christ, to strive ever more earnestly to promote this most gratifying devotion.

We are confident that in our day, as in others, a great many blessings will flow from it.

A DUTY OF RELIGION

Indeed, if the evidence on which devotion to the wounded heart of Jesus rests is rightly weighed, it is clear to all that we are dealing here, not with an ordinary form of piety which anyone may at his discretion esteem less than other devotions, or regard lightly, but with a duty of religion most conducive to Christian perfection.

For if devotion, according to the common theological definition which the Angelic Doctor gives, "is apparently nothing else but the will to give oneself readily to things concerning the service of God,"[110] can there be a service to God more required and necessary—and at the same time nobler and more pleasant—than that which pays homage to His love?

LOVE IS A FIRST GIFT

What is more pleasing and acceptable to God than that service which submits to divine love and is rendered for the sake of love, since every service freely rendered is, in a sense, a gift, and love "has the nature of a first gift in strength whereof all free gifts are given"?[111]

That form of religion must be held in highest honor by virtue of which man honors and loves God the more; by which he consecrates himself more easily and readily to divine love; and which our Redeemer Himself deigned to propose and recommend to Christianity and the Sovereign Pontiffs have defended in memorable writings and extolled with highest praise.

Therefore, whoever considers of little value this wonderful favor which Jesus Christ has bestowed upon His Church does a rash and harmful thing and offends God Himself.

"WITH YOUR WHOLE HEART"

In view of this, there is no doubt that the faithful who honor the Sacred Heart of the Redeemer comply with the very grave obligation by which they are bound to serve God; they dedicate themselves and all they have, both their inner thoughts and outward actions, to the Creator and Redeemer; and thus they obey the divine commandment: "You shall love the Lord your God with your whole heart, and with your whole soul, and with your whole mind, and with your whole strength."[112]

THE RIGHT UNDERSTANDING AND THE WRONG

In addition to this, they know with certainty that they are primarily led to worship God not for any personal advantage, be it spiritual or physical, temporal or eternal, but on account of the goodness of God, whom they strive to serve by loving Him in return, by adoring Him and by thanking Him.

If this were not true, devotion to the Sacred Heart of Jesus would not be in accord with the true nature of the Christian religion, since by such devotion divine love is not primarily venerated. And so, those who do not correctly understand the superior nature of this devotion or practice it in the wrong way are not unjustly, as sometimes happens, accused of excessive love and concern for themselves.

Let all therefore be firmly convinced that in showing devotion to the most august heart of Jesus external acts of piety do not play the first and foremost role. Nor is the reason for this devotion to be sought primarily in the blessings which Christ the Lord promised in private revelations in order that men might fulfill more fervently the principal duties of the Catholic Faith, namely, the obligations of love and expiation, and so be especially mindful of their own spiritual advancement.

CHERISH THIS DEVOTION

We therefore urge all our sons in Christ to cherish this form of devotion eagerly, both those who already are accustomed to drink the saving waters which flow from the heart of the Redeemer, and especially those who, in the idle manner of spectators, look on from a distance with misgivings.

Let them seriously consider that we speak of a devotion, as we have already said, which has long flourished in the Church and is firmly based on the Gospel and which tradition and the sacred liturgy openly encourage.

THE POPES SPEAK

The Roman Pontiffs themselves praised it most highly on numerous occasions, and were not content merely to institute a feast in honor of the august heart of the Redeemer and extend it to the universal Church, but also solemnly consecrated and dedicated the whole human race to the Sacred Heart.[113]

FRUITS OF THE DEVOTION

Finally, there are additional rich and joyous blessings which this devotion brings to the Church: the return of countless souls to the religion of Christ, the reanimated faith of many people and the closer union of the faithful with our most loving Redeemer. All of these, especially in recent decades, have appeared before our eyes in ever increasing and richer profusion.

GRATITUDE AND THANKSGIVING

As we look upon this marvelous spectacle of devotion to the Sacred Heart of Jesus, so widespread and so ardent among all classes of the faithful, we are filled with a gratifying and joyous sense of consolation.

After rendering fitting thanks to our Redeemer, who is the infinite treasure of goodness, we cannot refrain from extending our paternal congratulations to all, both of the clergy and of the laity, who have actively contributed to the spreading of this devotion.

THE TASK AHEAD

But even though devotion to the Sacred Heart of Jesus has everywhere produced the salutary fruits of Christian living, nonetheless, venerable brothers, it is clear that the Church Militant here on earth, and especially civil society, have not yet achieved that full and complete measure of perfection which corresponds to the wishes and desires of Jesus Christ, the Mystical Spouse of the Church and the Redeemer of the human race.

THE RETURN OF SINNERS

Not a few of the Church's children mar the beauty of their mother's countenance, which they reflect in themselves, with too many blemishes and wrinkles. Not all the faithful are resplendent with that sanctity of life to which they have been called by God.

All sinners have not returned to their Father's house, which they wrongly left, there to put on once more the *best robe*[114] and to receive for their finger a ring, the sign of fidelity to the Spouse of their soul.

THE CONVERSION OF PAGANS

Not all of the pagans, not even a goodly number, have yet been joined to the Mystical Body of Christ. For if we are caused bitter grief by the languishing faith of the good, whose souls have been led astray by a deceptive desire for worldly possessions so that the fervor of charity grows cold and is gradually extinguished, the machinations of the wicked wrack us with even greater pain.

As if goaded on by the infernal enemy, these men, especially now, are on fire with an implacable and open hatred for God, the Church, and especially for him who takes the place of the divine Redeemer on earth and represents His love for men according to the well-known words of St. Ambrose: "For [Peter] is questioned in a matter about which he feels uncertain; but the Lord who put the question has no doubt. He asked not to find out, but to point out before His ascension him whom *He left us as the Vicar of His love.*"[115]

THE GREATEST SIN

Indeed, hatred of God and those who lawfully take His place is so great a sin that man, created in the image and likeness of God and destined to enjoy His friendship which is to last forever in heaven, can commit none greater.

By hatred of God, man is separated completely from the highest good and driven to cast from himself and his fellow men whatever comes from God, whatever joins us to God and whatever leads us to enjoy God, that is, truth, virtue, peace and justice.[116]

Unfortunately, since it is possible to see increasing everywhere the number of those who glory in being enemies of God, the false tenets of *materialism* being propagated in practice and theory, and unbridled freedom of lust everywhere extolled, what wonder if charity—the supreme law of the Christian religion, the surest foundation of true and perfect justice, the chief source of peace and chaste pleasure—grow cold in the souls of many? For, as our Savior warned, "because iniquity will abound, the charity of the many will grow cold."[117]

THE REMEDY: DEVOTION TO THE SACRED HEART

In the face of so many evils which today more than ever deeply disturb individuals, homes, nations and the whole world, where, venerable brothers, is a remedy to be sought?

Is there a devotion more excellent than that to the Sacred Heart of Jesus, one which is more in accord with the real nature of the Catholic faith or which better meets the needs of the Church and the human race today? What act of religion is nobler, more suitable, sweeter and more conducive to salvation, since this devotion is wholly directed to the love of God Himself?[118]

Finally, what can bring the faithful to live the law of the Gospel more effectively than the love of Christ, which devotion to the Sacred Heart daily increases and fosters?

If this law is rejected, is it possible to have genuine peace among men? As the words of the Holy Spirit clearly teach, "The work of justice shall be peace."[119]

SOURCE AND STANDARD OF UNITY, SALVATION, PEACE

Therefore, following the example of our immediate predecessor, we choose to address again to all our beloved sons in Christ the words of admonition which Leo XIII of immortal memory spoke to all the faithful at the end of the last century. We likewise address these words to all who have a genuine concern for their own salvation and that of civil society. "Behold another most auspicious and divine standard presented to our view today: the Sacred Heart of Jesus gleaming with dazzling light, surrounded by flames. In it all hopes must be placed, in it man's salvation must be sought and looked for."[120]

It is also our most ardent desire that all who glory in the name of Christian and who zealously strive to establish the kingdom of Christ on earth consider devotion to the heart of Jesus as the standard and the source of unity, salvation and peace.

DOES NOT DETRACT FROM OTHER DEVOTIONS

Nevertheless, let no one think that this devotion detracts anything from other devotions with which Christian people, under the leadership of the Church, honor the divine Redeemer.

On the contrary, ardent devotion to the heart of Jesus will, without doubt, encourage and promote devotion to the most holy cross and love for the most august Sacrament of the altar. For we can definitely state a fact which the revelations made by Jesus Christ to St. Gertrude and St. Margaret Mary marvelously confirm: that no one ever fittingly loves Christ hanging on the cross but he to whom the mystical secrets of His Sacred Heart have been unfolded.

THE EUCHARISTIC HEART OF JESUS

Nor will it be easy to grasp the force of that love by which Christ was impelled to give Himself as our spiritual food except by fostering in a special way devotion to the Eucharistic heart of Jesus.

The purpose of this devotion, to use the words of our predecessor of happy memory, Leo XIII, is to recall to our minds "that supreme act of love by which our Redeemer, pouring forth all the riches of His heart, instituted the adorable sacrament of the Eucharist to remain in our midst to the end of time."[121]

For "not the smallest portion of His heart is the Eucharist which He gave us from the overflowing love of His heart."[122]

A SCHOOL OF DIVINE CHARITY

Finally, greatly impelled by the desire to set up a firm defense against the wicked machinations of the enemies of God and His Church, and at the same time to lead back domestic and civil society to the love of God and neighbor, we do not hesitate to state emphatically that devotion to the Sacred Heart of Jesus is a most effective school of divine love. On this love must rest the kingdom of God which is to be established in the souls of individuals, in families and in nations.

As our same predecessor of blessed memory most wisely teaches: "The kingdom of Jesus Christ draws its power and distinctive characteristics from divine love; its foundation and chief doctrine is to love holily and in proper order. From this it necessarily follows that we must fulfill obligations faithfully, detract nothing from the rights of others, consider human matters inferior to divine and place love of God above everything else."[123]

THE IMMACULATE HEART OF MARY

That graces for the Christian family and for the whole human race may flow more abundantly from devotion to the Sacred Heart, let the faithful strive to join it closely with devotion to the Immaculate Heart of the Mother of God.

By the will of God, the most Blessed Virgin Mary was inseparably joined with Christ in accomplishing the work of man's redemption, so that our salvation flows from the love of Jesus Christ and His sufferings, intimately united with the love and sorrows of His Mother.

It is, then, highly fitting that after due homage has been paid to the most Sacred Heart of Jesus, Christian people, who have obtained divine life from Christ through Mary, manifest for the most loving heart of our heavenly Mother similar affections of devotion, love and a spirit of gratitude and expiation.

The memorable act of consecration by which we ourselves, in the most wise and loving dispositions of divine Providence, solemnly dedicated the Church and the whole world to the untainted heart of the Blessed Virgin Mary, is in perfect accord with devotion to the Sacred Heart.[124]

CENTENARY OF THE FEAST OF THE SACRED HEART

Since in the course of the present year, as previously mentioned, we are joyfully completing the first century since our predecessor of happy memory, Pius IX, ordered the celebration of the feast of the most Sacred Heart of Jesus throughout the entire Church, it is our fervent desire, venerable brothers, that this centenary be solemnly celebrated by the faithful everywhere with public acts of adoration, thanksgiving and reparation to the divine heart of Jesus.

With all the faithful united in bonds of love and common prayer, these festivals of Christian joy and piety will be celebrated with special religious fervor in that country where by God's special providence the holy virgin who was the promoter and indefatigable herald of this devotion was born.

In the meantime, strengthened with joyous hope and in spirit already anticipating the spiritual fruits which we are certain will grow abundantly in the Church from devotion to the Sacred Heart, if correctly understood according to our explanation and zealously practiced, we humbly pray God lovingly to grant His grace for the fulfillment of our most ardent desire.

With God's help may this year's celebration increase from day to day the love of the faithful for the most Sacred Heart of Jesus. And may His kingdom, a kingdom "of truth and life, a kingdom of holiness and grace, a kingdom of justice, love and peace,"[125] be extended further to all in the whole world.

As a pledge of these heavenly graces, we most lovingly impart to each of you, venerable brothers, to the clergy and people entrusted to your care, and in particular to those who zealously encourage and promote devotion to the most Sacred Heart of Jesus, our apostolic benediction.

Given at Rome from St. Peter's, May 15, 1956, in the eighteenth year of our Pontificate.

PIUS PP. XII

1. *Is.* 12:3.
2. *Jas.* 1:17.
3. *Jn.* 7:37-39. The Holy Father's text here and in a few other places differs from the Vulgate.—Ed.
4. Cf. *Is.* 12:3; *Ez.* 47:1-12; *Za.* 13:1; *Ex.* 17:1-7; *Nm.* 20:7-13; *1 Cor.* 10:4; *Rev.* 7:17; 22:1.
5. *Rom.* 5:5.
6. *1 Cor.* 6:17.
7. *Jn.* 4:10.
8. Enc. *Annum Sacrum,* May 25, 1899: *Acta Leonis,* vol. 19, 1900, pp. 71, 77-78.
9. Enc. *Miserentissimus Redemptor,* May 8, 1928: *Acta Apostolicae Sedis* 20, 1928, p. 167.
10. Cf. Encyclical *Summi Pontificatus,* October 20, 1939: *Acta Apostolicae Sedis* 31, 1939, p. 415.
11. Cf. *Acta Apostolicae Sedis* 32, 1940, p. 276; 35, 1943, p. 470; 37, 1945, pp. 263-264; 40, 1948, p. 501; 41, 1949, p. 331.
12. *Eph.* 3:20-21.
13. *Is.* 12:3.
14. Council of Ephesus, Can. 8; cf. Mansi, *Sacrorum Conciliorum Ampliss. Collectio,* 4, 1083 C; Second Council of Constantinople, can. 9; cf. *Ibid.* 9, 382 E.
15. Cf. Encl. *Annum Sacrum: Acta Leonis,* vol. 19, 1900, p. 76.
16. Cf. *Ex.* 34:27-28.
17. *Dt.* 6:4-6.
18. *Summa Theologica,* II-II, q. 2, a. 7: ed. Leon. tom. 8, 1895, p. 34.
19. *Dt.* 32:11.
20. *Hos.* 11:1, 3-4; 14, 5-6.

21. *Is.* 49:14-15.
22. *Ct.* 2:2; 6:2; 8:6.
23. *Jn.* 1:14.
24. *Jer.* 31:3, 31, 33-34.
25. *Jn.* 1:29; *Heb.* 9:18-28; 10:1-17.
26. *Jn.* 1:16-17.
27. *Jn.* 21:20.
28. *Eph.* 3:17-19.
29. *Summa Theologica* III, q. 48, a. 2: ed. Leon. tom. 11, 1903, p. 464.
30. Cf. Encyclical *Miserentissimus Redemptor: Acta Apostolicae Sedis* 20, 1928, p. 170.
31. *Summa Theologica* III, q. 48, a. 1 ad 3: ed. Leon. tom. 11, 1903, p. 436. *Eph.* 2:4.
32. *Eph.* 3:18.
33. *Jn.* 4:24.
34. *2 Jn.* 7.
35. Cf. *Lk.* 1:35.
36. St. Leo the Great, *Epist. Dogm. "Lectis dilectionis tuae" ad Flavianum Const. Patr.* June 13, a. 449; cf. *P.L.* LIV, 763.
37. Council of Chalcedon, a. 451; cf. Mansi, *op cit.* 7, 115 B.
38. Pope St. Gelasius, Tract, 3: *"Necessarium," Of the Two Natures in Christ,* cf. A. Thiel, *Letters of the Roman Pontiffs from St. Hilary to Pelagius II,* p. 532.
39. Cf. St. Thomas, *Summa Theologica* III, q. 15, a. 4; q. 18, a. 6: ed. Leon. tom. 11, 1903, p. 189 and 237.
40. Cf. *1 Cor.* 1:23.
41. *Heb.* 2:11-14; 17-18.
42. *Apol.* 2:13: *P.G.* VI, 465.
43. *Epist.* 261, 3: *P.G.* XXXII, 972.
44. *In Joann. Homil.* 63, 2: *P.G.* LIX, 350.
45. *De fide ad Gratianum,* II, 7, 56: *P.L.* XVI, 594.
46. *Super Matth.* 26, 37: *P.L.* XXVI, 205.
47. *Enarr. in Ps.* 87, 3; *P.L.* XXXVII, 1111.
48. *De Fide Orth.* 3, 6: *P.G.* XCIV, 1006.
49. *Ibid.* 3, 20: *P.G.* XCIV, 1081.
50. *Summa Theologica,* I-II, q. 48, a. 4: ed. Leon. tom. 6, 1891, p. 306.
51. *Col.* 2:9.
52. Cf. *Summa Theologica,* III, q. 9, aa. 1-3: ed. Leon. tom. 11, 1903, p. 142.
53. Cf. *Ibid.,* III, q. 33, a. 2, ad 3m; q. 46, a. 6: ed. Leon. tom. 11, 1903, pp. 342, 433.
54. *Tit.* 3:4.
55. *Mt.* 27:50; *Jn.* 19:30.
56. *Eph.* 2:7.
57. *Heb.* 10:5-7, 10.
58. *Registr. epist.* lib. IV ep. 31 *ad Theodorum Medicum: P.L.* LXXVII, 706.
59. *Mk.* 8:2.
60. *Mt.* 23:37.
61. *Mt.* 21:13.
62. *Mt.* 26:39.
63. *Mt.* 26:50; *Lk.* 22:48.
64. *Lk.* 23:28, 31.
65. *Lk.* 23:24.
66. *Mt.* 27:46.
67. *Lk.* 23:43.
68. *Jn.* 19:28.
69. *Lk.* 23:46.
70. *Lk.* 22:15.
71. *Lk.* 22:19-20.

72. *Mal.* 1:11.
73. *De Sancta Virginitate,* VI: *P.L.* XL, 399.
74. *Jn.* 15:13.
75. *1 Jn.* 3:16.
76. *Gal.* 2:20.
77. Cf. St. Thomas, *Sum. Theol.* III, q. 19, a. 1: ed. Leon. tom. XI, 1903, p. 329.
78. *Sum. Theol. Suppl.* q. 42, a. 1 ad 3m: ed. Leon. tom. XII, 1906, p. 81.
79. Hymn *ad Vesp. Festi SSmi. Cordis Jesu.*
80. *Sum. Theol.* III, q. 66, a. 3 ad 3m: ed. Leon. tom. XII, 1906, p. 65.
81. *Eph.* 5:2.
82. *Eph.* 4:8, 10.
83. *Jn.* 14:16.
84. *Col.* 2:3.
85. *Rom.* 8:35, 37-39.
86. *Eph.* 5:25-27.
87. Cf. *1 Jn.* 2:1.
88. *Heb.* 7:25.
89. *Heb.* 5:7.
90. *Jn.* 3:16.
91. St. Bonaventure, Opusc. X: *Vitis mystica,* c. III, n. 5; *Opera Omnia,* Ad Claras Aquas (Quararachi), 1898, tom. VIII, p. 164; cf. St. Thomas, *Sum. Theol.* III, q. 54, a. 4: ed. Leon. tom. XI, 1903, p. 513.
92. *Rom.* 8:32.
93. Cf. *Summa Theologica* III, q. 48, a. 5; ed. Leon. tom. 11, 1903, p. 467.
94. *Lk.* 12:50.
95. *Jn.* 20:28.
96. *Jn.* 19:37; cf. *Za.* 12:10.
97. Cf. Enc. *Miserentissimus Redemptor: Acta Apostolicae Sedis* 20, 1928, pp. 167-168.
98. Cf. A. Gardellini, *Decreta authentica,* 1857, n. 4579, tom. 3, p. 174.
99. Cf. *Decr. S.C. Rit.* apud N. Nilles *De rationibus festorum Sacratissimi Cordis Jesu et purissimi Cordis Mariae,* 5th edition, Innsbruck, 1885, tom. 1, p. 167.
100. *Eph.* 3:14, 16-19.
101. *Ti.* 3:4.
102. *Jn.* 3:17.
103. *Jn.* 4:23-24.
104. Innocent XI, Constit. Ap. *Coelestis Pastor,* November 19, 1687; *Bullarium Romanum,* Rome, 1734, tom. 8, p. 443.
105. *Sum. Theol.* II-II, q. 81, a. 3 ad 3m: ed. Leon. tom. 9, 1897, p. 180.
106. *Jn.* 14:6.
107. *Jn.* 13:34; 15:12.
108. *Jn.* 31:31.
109. *Comment. in Evang. S. Joann.* c. 13, lect. 7, 3: ed. Parmae, 1869, tom. 10, p. 541.
110. *Sum. Theol.* II-II, q. 82, a. 1.
111. *Sum. Theol.* I, q. 38, a. 2.
112. *Mk.* 12:30; *Mt.* 22:37.
113. Cf. Leo XIII, Enc. *Annum Sacrum: Acta Leonis,* vol. 19, 1900, p. 71 sq.; *Decr. S.C. Rituum,* June 28, 1899, in *Decr. Auth.* 3, n. 3712; Pius XI, Enc. *Miserentissimus Redemptor: Acta Apostolicae Sedis,* 1928, p. 177 sq.; *Decr. S.C. Rit.,* January 29, 1929: *Acta Apostolicae Sedis* 21, 1929, p. 77.
114. *Lk.* 15:22.
115. *Exposit. in Evang. sec. Lucam,* 1, 10, n. 175; *P.L.* XV, 1942.
116. Cf. St. Thomas, *Sum. Theol.* II-II, q. 34, a. 2: ed. Leon. tom. 8, 1895, p. 274.

117. *Mt.* 24:12.

118. Cf. Enc. *Miserentissimus Redemptor: Acta Apostolicae Sedis* 20, 1928, p. 166.

119. *Is.* 32:17.

120. Enc. *Annum Sacrum: Acta Leonis*, vol. 19, 1900, p. 79; *Miserentissimus Redemptor: Acta Apostolicae Sedis* 20, 1928, p. 167.

121. *Litt. Apost. Quibus Archisodalitas a Corde Eucharistico Jesu ad S. Joachim de Urbe erigitur*, February 17, 1903: *Acta Leonis*, vol. 22, 1903, p. 307 sq.; cf. Enc. *Mirae caritatis*, May 22, 1902: *Acta Leonis*, vol. 22, 1903, p. 116.

122. St. Albert the Great, *De Eucharistia*, dist. 6, tr. 1, c. 1: *Opera Omnia*, ed. Borgnet, vol. 38, Paris, 1890, p. 358.

123. Enc. *Tametsi: Acta Leonis*, vol. 20, 1900, p. 303.

124. Cf. *Acta Apostolicae Sedis* 34, 1942, p. 345 sq.

125. Roman Missal *Preface of Jesus Christ the King*.

ADDITIONAL LIVES OF SAINTS AVAILABLE:

Heavenly Friends, A Saint for Each Day

Rosalie Marie Levy

A superb book, epitomizing the lives of more than 400 famous saints.

486 pages; deluxe $7.00; cloth or plastic $5.00; paper $4.00

Joseph, the Just Man

Rosalie Marie Levy

A complete biography, supplemented with accounts of favors granted and selections of special prayers.

285 pages; cloth $4.00; paper $3.00

Joseph: The Man Closest to Jesus

Francis L. Filas, SJ

Never before has all this wealth of intensely interesting and little-known facts about St. Joseph been compiled into a single book. This can truly be called a "little Summa" of St. Joseph, as the only survey existing in any language of the complete life, theology, and devotional history of St. Joseph.

682 pages; cloth $6.50; paper $5.50

The Legacy of St. Patrick

Martin P. Harney, SJ

The legacy of St. Patrick, which he would bequeath to his brethren and their descendants, was his own holy idealism. It can be found in his two writings, the Confession of St. Patrick and the Letters to the Soldiers of Coroticus.

A thoughtful perusal of the Confession and of the Letter will reward the reader with a true and an intimate knowledge of St. Patrick.

148 pages; cloth $3.00

Order from addresses on last page.

Magnificent Witnesses

Martin P. Harney, SJ

Simple, heart-warming, soul-stirring sketches of the English and Welsh martyrs, canonized by Pope Paul VI on October 25, 1970. The martyrs included 13 secular priests, 20 religious (of 5 orders), 4 laymen and 3 laywomen. All gave their lives for the fundamental doctrine of the Primacy of the Pope.

80 pages; cloth $2.00

St. Gemma, the Passion Flower

Msgr. Joseph Bardi

A touching biography, the memory of which will be a source of consolation in time of suffering.

182 pages; cloth $2.00

St. Joan of Arc, Virgin—Soldier

Msgr. Leon Cristiani

The author scrupulously strives to present the simple, naked, historical truth about the life and times of Joan of Arc. He also outlines the supernatural in Joan's life in all its clarity.

160 pages; cloth $4.00; paper $3.00

St. Martin de Porres

Richard Cardinal Cushing

For forty-five years St. Martin dedicated himself almost entirely to the performance of spiritual and corporal works of mercy. "A thumbnail sketch in which the 'digitus Dei' clearly appears in the life and work of St. Martin." "Central California Register"

80 pages; cloth $1.50

Order from addresses on last page.

Mother Seton—wife, mother, educator, foundress, saint

Daughters of St. Paul

This fast-paced life of "an authentic daughter of America" (Pope John's term) is completed by selections from Mother Seton's own writings —Spiritual Gems—that permit us to glimpse the deep spirituality of the first American-born saint.

140 pages; cloth $3.95; paper $2.95

Saint of the Impossible

Daughters of St. Paul

Fast-paced chapters tell of St. Rita's childhood and youth, of her will to succeed in her stormy marriage, of the transformation worked in her husband by her prayer and suffering for him, of her two sons, their death and her widowed loneliness. Even St. Rita's desire for religious life was thwarted at first, but the belief in God's unfailing care never left her... and she succeeded.

104 pages; cloth $3.95

St. Paul, Apostle and Martyr

Igino Giordani

St. Paul inspires many a modern-day laborer, housewife, intellectual, businessman, politician and statesman to bring God's kingdom to all. "What the author desired—the presentation of a living, human Paul—he admirably achieved." "Catholic Book Reporter"

38 full-color illustrations and 33 in black and white.

392 pages; deluxe $9.00; cloth $7.00; paper $6.00

Order from addresses on last page.

St. Teresa of Avila

Giorgio Papasogli

It took the author a year's visit to Spain, exhaustive research and an intensive study of all the existing material before he was ready to write. The result was an entirely new biography of one of the most written-about women in the world.

410 pages; cloth $5.00

St. Theresa, the Little Flower

Sister Gesualda of the Holy Spirit

The heart-warming story of a modern saint known and venerated the world over!

270 pages; cloth $4.00; paper $3.00

Three Ways of Love

Frances Parkinson Keyes

The world-famous author here captures the romance, the tragedy and the history of three great women: St. Agnes, whose name has become synonymous with courage; St. Frances of Rome, a mother and the protectress of the poor and sick; and St. Catherine of Siena, the famous ambassadress and stateswoman.

304 pages; cloth $6.00; paper $5.00

Order from addresses on last page.

Sisters,
Please send me:

____

____

____

name ______________________________

address ______________________________

city ______________ state ______________ zip ________

Enclosed is my payment for $______________

Daughters of St. Paul

IN MASSACHUSETTS
50 St. Paul's Avenue, Boston, Ma. 02130
172 Tremont Street, Boston, Ma. 02111
IN NEW YORK
78 Fort Place, Staten Island, N.Y. 10301
625 East 187th Street, Bronx, N.Y. 10458
525 Main Street, Buffalo, N.Y. 14203
IN NEW JERSEY
84 Washington Street, Bloomfield, N.J. 07003
IN CONNECTICUT
202 Fairfield Avenue, Bridgeport, Ct. 06603
IN OHIO
2105 Ontario St. (at Prospect Ave.), Cleveland, Oh. 44115
25 E. Eighth Street, Cincinnati, Oh. 45202
IN PENNSYLVANIA
1719 Chestnut St., Philadelphia, Pa. 19103
IN FLORIDA
2700 Biscayne Blvd., Miami, Fl. 33137
IN LOUISIANA
4403 Veterans Memorial Blvd.,
Metairie, La. 70002
86 Bolton Avenue, Alexandria, La. 71301
IN MISSOURI
1001 Pine St. (at North 10th), St. Louis, Mo. 63101
IN TEXAS
114 East Main Plaza, San Antonio, Tx. 78205
IN CALIFORNIA
1570 Fifth Avenue, San Diego, Ca. 92101
278 17th Street, Oakland, Ca. 94612
46 Geary Street, San Francisco, Ca. 94108
IN HAWAII
1184 Bishop St., Honolulu, Hi. 96813
IN ALASKA
5th Ave. and H. St.
Anchorage, Ak. 99501
IN CANADA
3022 Dufferin Street, Toronto 395, Ontario, Canada
IN ENGLAND
57, Kensington Church Street, London W. 8, England
IN AUSTRALIA
58, Abbotsford Rd., Homebush, N.S.W., Sydney 2140,
Australia

Order from
TAN Books & Publishers
P. O. Bo[illegible] 24
Rockford, Illin[illegible] 61105